"The perfect tool for preparing and sustaining anyone sensing the call to a short-term mission project. It is both intensely practical and deeply spiritual as it provides advice for the emotional experience of sending our best out on mission for the first time."

—Michael Card
Best-selling recording artist, songwriter, and author

HOW TO GET READY FOR
SHORT-TERM
MISSIONS

HOW TO GET READY FOR
SHORT-TERM
MISSIONS

THE ULTIMATE GUIDE FOR SPONSORS, PARENTS AND

THOSE WHO GO!

Anne-Geri' Fann
& GREG TAYLOR

THOMAS NELSON
Since 1798

NASHVILLE   DALLAS   MEXICO CITY   RIO DE JANEIRO   BEIJING

Published in Nashville, Tennessee, by Thomas Nelson, Inc.

Nelson books may be purchased in bulk for educational, business, fundraising, or sales promotion use. For information, please email SpecialMarkets@ThomasNelson.com.

Nelson books may also be purchased in bulk for ministry use by churches, parachurch ministries, and media ministries. For information, please call (800) 251-4000 ext. 2804 or email NelsonMinistryServices@thomasnelson.com.

Unless otherwise noted, Scripture quotations are from the HOLY BIBLE: NEW INTERNATIONAL VERSION®. Copyright © 1973, 1978, 1984 by International Bible Society. Used by permission of Zondervan Publishing House. All rights reserved.

Scripture quotations noted NASB are from the NEW AMERICAN STANDARD BIBLE®, © Copyright the Lockman Foundation 1960, 1962, 1963, 1968, 1971, 1972, 1973, 1975, 1977. Used by permission. www.Lockman.org

Managing Editors Michael Christopher and W. Mark Whitlock
Edited by Steffany Woolsey
Book packaging by Design Point, Inc.
Interior design by Kristy Morell

Library of Congress Cataloging-in-Publication Data
Fann, Anne-Geri', 1968-
How to get ready for short-term missions : a survival guide / Anne-Geri'
Fann and Greg Taylor.
p. cm.
Includes bibliographical references.
ISBN 978-1-4185-0977-4 (pbk.)
1. Short-term missions. I. Taylor, Greg, 1967- II. Title.
BV2082.S56F36 2006
266.0023--dc22
2006007603

Printed in Canada
07 08 09 10 11 12 TC 9 8 7 6 5 4 3 2

CONTENTS

ACKNOWLEDGMENTS

We want to thank our editors, Michael Christopher and Steffany Woolsey, who not only saw the great need for this book but also rolled up their sleeves and turned it inside out, helping transform it into a book that might reach the hearts of young people and mission leaders. Thank you to Les Middleton and Mark Whitlock as well. Your enthusiasm for this book on missions is life-giving to us.

To parents of short-term missionaries who helped us in research, both those whose input appears in the book and those whose opinions did not, we thank you. To the missionaries who graciously wrote advice for the book, much of which is included, we are grateful. Both senders and goers on mission trips are an inspiration to us and have provided loads of great stories and principles.

Thank you to Sam S. Adams, Carlos and Amy Alfaro, Craig Altrock, Mark Berryman, Johnny and Wanda Bizzell, Ginger Brown, David and Suyapa Chacón, Doris Clark, Melaney Cost, Monte Cox, Mike and Molly Dawidow, Clint Davis, Matt and Lela Elliott, David H. Fann, Jeff and Janna Gilbert, Stan Granberg, Glen and Anne Gray, Ryan and Amanda Gray, Pat Gray, Joe Glenn, Adilia Guillen, Alan and Lanita Henderson, Kyle Huhtanen, Shirley and Susan Jones, Jason and Amy Laffan, Pat Lamb, Amanda Madrid, Steve Meeks, Fernando Nasmyth, Norberto Otero, Juana Elia Romero Ponce, Sam Shewmaker, Jill Taylor, Charlie Walton, Robert and Miriam Warner, Mark Willis, Greg Williams, Kim Wirgau, and Mark and Brenda Young. Many of these deserve our gratitude for holding our hands through this book, while some may not even be aware that they inspired it. Others are now with Jesus and we can't wait to be with them someday; we want to be where you are.

DEDICATION

This book is dedicated to my dad.

When I think of how the desire to "do missions" was instilled in my heart, some very clear images come to mind.

The first image is this mimeographed copy of a song typed on an old Remington Rand typewriter, a piece of paper pasted in one of my college textbooks, still on my shelf. They are the words to a song written for a young missionary couple by some brothers and sisters in Lubbock, Texas. A group of children at their going-away party belted it out to the tune of "Battle Hymn of the Republic." It was a departure song, a blessing sung over Glen and Anne Gray, my parents, as they prepared to go to New Zealand for the first time.

In the second image, as in a dream, I am my mother on a beautiful New Zealand afternoon. I am looking out from the back porch at my daughter, who is swinging from a grapefruit tree in a big tire. I am listening to that wide-eyed four-year-old sing loudly (and off-key) the chorus to the same song.

I always wondered why I see this image as my mother would see it. Now I realize that I am her in so many ways. And I know she taught me that song for a reason.

The third image is the Koine Greek grammar book that I had in college. My dad wrote notes all over it while *he* was in college. In addition, I wrote around and on top of all his notes. The grammar tells the story of a father's desire to learn the Word of God and plant it in his heart. It also tells how he deeply engrained that love for the Word in his daughter's heart, and how she grew to desire the knowledge of eternity. Yes, it is the same textbook I mentioned before—the one with the song pasted on the inside cover. Here, finally, is the song:

I can go to North Dakota, I can go to Timbuktu.
I can climb the highest mountain; I can cross the ocean blue.
I can go and teach the Indian; I can teach the Chinese, too
And save the souls of men.

Chorus:
I can be a missionary; I can be a missionary
I can be a missionary, and save the souls of men!

On a ship next December to New Zealand they will go,
Brother Gray and nineteen others to that land that lies below.
They will tell the simple story of how Jesus loves them so
And save the souls of men.

(Chorus)

I will give the church my pennies and my nickels and my dimes.
Every morning, noon and evening, I will pray for them each time;
That they will preach the gospel and be gentle, pure, and kind
And save the souls of men.

(Chorus)

And when I am big and grown up to New Zealand I will go
Or some other land where people have not heard and do not know
That Jesus bled and died for them because He loved them so
And to save the souls of men!

(Chorus)

The song may sound cheesy, and some parts may not be too PC these days. But I can't read the last verse without a lump in my throat. I wasn't there to hear the children sing this song, but their voices ring out regardless. I think it is beautiful.

So yes, the fourth image is of my dad. My dad, preaching on a grass mat in Tonga. My dad, baptizing Mark Willis, who became a preacher and is now a professor at New Zealand Bible College. My dad, wielding a machete in Honduras as he gives a gospel lesson (I can't remember the point he was trying to make, but my Honduran friends got a kick out of the gringo with the machete). My dad, balancing a broom perfectly with one finger and looking up at the top, to prove to me that in order to keep life in balance, one must always look to the Lord. My dad, talking to his neighbor about Jesus. Not forcefully, but lovingly—"gentle, pure, and kind," as the song says.

Did I mention where he was while doing this? In New Zealand, in Louisiana, in Texas, in Colorado, in Nebraska, in Iowa, in Honduras, in Tennessee, in Jamaica, in the checkout line at Albertson's . . .

Thank you, Dad, for teaching me to be a missionary on whatever path my life is led. And thank you for teaching me to *be* led. And thanks, Mom and Dad, for my name. May it always honor you and the One you serve.

"So when I am big and grown up to New Zealand I will go, or some other land where people have not heard and do not know that Jesus bled and died for them because He loved them so . . ."

O for a faith that will not shrink,

Anne-Geri'

DEDICATION

My wife, Jill, and I decided to commit years to church planting in Uganda only after our close friends, John and Sara Barton, "called a huddle." They said, "We're going to Uganda. We really want you to go with us. But we're going no matter what."

We decided to join a vision that was bigger than ourselves. When we told our parents, they both said something similar and equally blessed us: "We will desperately miss you (and our grandchildren), but we support you . . . and we will come visit you."

They did come—for a combined total of ten visits. Unlike Angie, my parents and my wife's parents were not missionaries—but they are probably like most parents who will read this book: They desire for their children to experience a mission bigger than themselves, to live God's love, and to share it with the world.

To my parents, Terrel and Charlotte Taylor, and to Jill's parents, Ray and Bobbie Smiley, and to all my mission teammates, thank you.

Survival Guide Schedule

Chapter Title	Best Time to Read
Introduction	as soon as you have made the decision to go
(1) *The Journey Begins*	as soon as you have made the decision to go
(2) *Things to Pack*	a month before you go
(3) *Entering a Foreign Culture*	two weeks before you go
(4) *What You Have to Offer*	right before your trip
(5) *What You Don't Want to Offer*	on the plane or van or bus
(6) *Building Relationships*	immediately after your arrival (or perhaps the next morning during your reflection time); read again when you return home
(7) *What to Expect When You Return Home*	on the trip home
(8) *For the Folks: Kicking Your Kids Out of the Family Tree*	for the parents to read as soon as you have made the decision to go

INTRODUCTION

This guide was written for *you.*

Preparation is necessary. Short-term mission work is rapidly growing in popularity for church youth groups and ministry teams. Many Christians agree that mission trips are helpful but admit that lack of preparedness—both cultural and spiritual—can hinder the true mission.

Our greatest need in Christianity is not necessarily for more short-term mission work, but for generating future missionaries and mission supporters through that exposure. This travel guide will direct and challenge you on topics like culture, flexibility, what you do and don't have to offer, the biblical basis for mission work, relationships on the field, and ways to discover and use your gifts on your trip.

Approximately two million North Americans will go on short-term missions this year. Hundreds of thousands of these are teenagers who will be swinging hammers and pounding nails in places like Juarez, Mexico, and Choluteca, Honduras.

Perhaps you too are riding the wave of mission-trip popularity . . . yet a nagging voice in your mind says you need more preparation. Have you stopped to wonder if the people you will be serving want you to build for them? Have you or your leader asked what they really need? These are examples of questions we'll prompt you to ask.

Each chapter in this book begins with a real-life story, called a **Missionary Moment,** which will set the tone for the chapter and prompt discussion. And at the close of each chapter you'll find an **Eternal Endeavor**—an activity designed to help you imagine and act on what it would be like for *you* to be a missionary.

Whether it be short-term or for a lifetime, a missionary's ultimate goal of reaching people has more to do with building relationships than making contacts. In order to do this, one must endeavor to be wholly like Jesus, who was gentle, pure, and kind; who hung out with the "untouchables"; who valued every individual He encountered; and who taught us how to truly love one another.

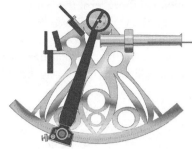

THE JOURNEY BEGINS 1

Missionary Moment ...

Charles Plumb, a U.S. Naval Academy graduate, was a jet fighter pilot in Vietnam. One day his plane was hit by a surface-to-air missile and Charles had to parachute to safety . . . sort of. He was captured and spent six years in a Communist prison. He now travels to lecture about the lessons he learned from that experience.

One day, when Charles and his wife were sitting in a restaurant, a man at another table came up and said, "You're Plumb! You flew jet fighters in Nam from the carrier Kitty Hawk. You were shot down!"

"How in the world did you know that?" asked Charles.

"I was the one who packed your parachute," the man replied.

Fingers twiddle. Hearts race. Lumps form in throats. Suitcases fill up. Passports are pulled out of hiding. It is almost time. So how do you feel? Maybe you want to go on this trip but find yourself reviewing your purpose in the adventure. Maybe you are excited about sharing your culture and understanding with those of another worldview. Or maybe you'll admit to going along for the ride and you're not necessarily tripping over yourself to get onto the plane.

You can hear it, can't you? The countdown. You've prayed about it, you've weighed the pros and cons, you've consulted your loved ones, you've looked at maps, and you've listened to missionaries . . . now it is time to take the exciting plunge into short-term mission work.

Whatever your feelings, please let me first encourage you in this way: *You are doing a good thing.* God is moving in this world. His kingdom is growing in parts of the world you have never been, places of which you have never heard. His great arm is touching the nations, speaking to them in ways you may never comprehend. He is desperate to move His created into a deeper relationship with Him. You are one of those. You accepted His great arm and embraced Him. Now you are commissioned to *go.* And you are going. But let's not plunge in without packing a proverbial parachute!

A worldview is one of the most important elements of your trip.

Mission trips need focused preparation, even if it is a short-term trip. There are some who believe that all we need to do is just *go!* Yes, trips have been done that way—where the only serious planning was to buy plane tickets and make sure everyone has his or her passport. Those trips can be fruitful. But in all honesty, they are rewarding mainly for the ones who are going, not necessarily the people who they are going to serve.

After meeting the man who packed his parachute, Charles Plumb was forced to ponder how much time the sailor had spent in the depths of the Kitty Hawk, carefully folding each chute. Did he realize that each time he did so, he held in his hands the fate of someone he did not know?

Today Charles challenges his audiences with the question, "Who is packing your chute?" He reminds his audience that four different kinds of parachutes are needed—mental, emotional, spiritual, and physical. While a prisoner of war, Charles called on each of these supports before finally reaching safety.[1] Who packed *our* parachutes? Are we ready to take a leap of faith into a joyous journey, or are we headed for short-term disaster?

In March 2000, the maker of the Zenit 3-SL booster rocket, which had a disastrous takeoff from a platform in the Pacific, had to publicize the fact that an error in the prelaunch sequence had caused the failure.[2] You don't want your mission team's goals to be unsuccessful due to faulty planning, do you?

Of course not; that is why you are reading this book. You want to cover all your bases. You know there's no way to know everything before you go, but you want to do your best to be aware of what is ahead of you, as well as be *ready* for challenges to your worldview.

> *Sociologist Christian Smith estimates that some two million North American thirteen- to seventeen-year-olds go on short-term trips domestically or internationally every year—and that's a conservative estimate![3] Many do great humanitarian work and often make some spiritual impact, but others, through lack of preparation and/or training, do more harm than good.*

You may be thinking, *Worldview? What on earth is that?* Let me tell you, it is one of the most important elements of your trip. Not too unlike a collection of stuffed animals or coins or baseball cards, a worldview is a collection of beliefs about life and the universe as held by a human being (or sometimes a group of people). It is the perspective from which an individual observes and understands the world.

And it is a good place to start.

Upside Down/Right Side Up

Because the first mapmakers were from Europe and America, they naturally drew themselves on the top. However, when you view the world from space, you see *Africa* on top.

Perspective can change in a moment. In much the same way, your worldview may change as you make this journey. This doesn't mean you will eventually see the earth from outer space, but you will more than likely take a step back and learn something that will surprise you, maybe even shake your foundation.

Some customs will be easy to understand, like the fact that Central Americans don't fancy personal space like North Americans do. Other differences may make your eyes pop: *It's okay for women to breastfeed in church in this African village? Men can hold hands as simply friends?*

Don't be scared of cultural differences or new ways of thinking; instead, look at them as adventures. Seeing things from a whole new angle can be a blessing.

I took one girl to Honduras who had issues with germs. Not her own germs, mind you; just everyone else's. She was especially reluctant to be touched on the hand. She would not join hands in prayer, hold hands with a boyfriend, or shake hands with strangers—it drove her mad to even think of it. Only her best friends knew about this phobia, and they confided in me about it before our trip. They were afraid the Latin American touchy-feely issue would freak her out.

Long story short, it didn't. By the end of the week she was letting little village girls drag her by both hands down the dirt road to the river, giggling all the way. I won't say it was easy for her, but here's what she told me afterward: "It was worth every germ."

The things you learn on this trip will be worth every penny, every prayer, every perspective-changing moment, every step. And at the end of the day, they will be worth every germ. Perhaps even the ones *you* are spreading!

It's Time!

It may be a bumpy ride, much like being squeezed into a fifteen-passenger van and heading up a windy dirt road toward a remote mountain village. On the other hand, it could be smooth sailing—like a plan that goes off without a glitch. The important thing to remember is that this is your opportunity to serve God's children in a different way.

In the words of one of our missionary mentors, you are doing something "bigger than yourself." Going on a short-term mission is a way to learn about the incredible world and humanity God created.

A final caution: Remember that God's "bigness" includes the fact that He's already been to Africa, Europe, and Asia. In fact, He's been to every place in every corner of the world. You're not taking God *to* them; God has been there all along.

He's only been waiting for you to come participate in *His mission.* So pack your proverbial parachute and let's take a leap of faith into the great adventure that is short-term mission work!

ETERNAL ENDEAVORS_____

Answer these questions as soon as you've made the decision to go. The more you put into answering them, the more they will help you.

1. Where are you going on your trip? _____

2. Think ahead. Take the time to find out some information about your target mission:
    a. Look at maps.
    b. Talk to people who have been there.
    c. Understand how the currency system works before you go.

Answer some of the following questions, and take the rest with you to ask the locals. They will be happy to tell you about their country, and it will strengthen your communication skills.

Things to Find out Before You Go

1. How do you plan to get there?

2. Is it a difficult place to reach?

3. Where do you plan to stay?

4. What means of transportation will you use while there?

5. What are some of the major cultural differences compared to what you are used to?

6. What other places will you visit around the area of your target mission?

7. What are the main occupations, and why are they prevalent in your country?

8. Does this society rely mainly on farming, business, tourism, or other? Why? How did it become that way? (Note: If you discover in advance the answer to this last question, you will really impress the people you travel with!)

9. Are there any environmental problems?

10. How big is this country? Which U.S. state (or Canadian province) does it most closely resemble in size?

11. What is the currency of this country? For what or who is it named?

12. What is the official language? Are there any less predominant languages?

13. Are any specific words or phrases standard for this time of year? Any special songs?

14. What are the main religions, and what role does religion play in the every-day lives of the people?

15. Are the nationally recognized holidays a reflection of the main religion (or lack of religion)?

Questions/Observations for During the Mission

Take this book with you as a journal and quick-reference tool. We've included several pages in the back for you.

1. Take note of any unusual billboards or street signs. Sketch them in your journal.

2. Ask about any buildings, structures, or monuments that look important. Ask a national (what we sometimes call "locals"—the term *native* is acceptable only when someone refers to himself as a "native" of a certain place) what they represent. Write about them in your journal.

3. Is there anything unusual about the plumbing at your target mission? Is there a reason for its condition (be it poor or exceptional)?

4. Ask about the political parties. Are there similarities to the political parties you are familiar with?

5. Is there anything different about the house and building construction?

6. Which side of the road do they drive on?

7. What kinds of things do you see (just passing by) that are similar, yet different from what you are accustomed to?

8. Find out as much as you can about their school systems. Do they have year-round school? Do they wear uniforms?

9. What are some favorite holidays or sports activities?

10. What is the meaning of the name of this country?

THINGS TO PACK *2*

Missionary Moment ...

In 1998, a group of teens in a small village in El Salvador was helping a campesino (farmer) rebuild his house after Hurricane Mitch had torn through the area. The farmer estimated how big he would like the house. It needed to be set in a deep foundation, and the group had only one pickax.

Taking turns, the teens dug a trench on the inside of the measuring wire in one perfect square. This took six hours (and included many water breaks).

Finally, the owner returned with the adobe bricks, looked at the layout of his house, and humbly said, "I did not calculate correctly. I am so sorry. I have many children. We need to dig the trench a few feet outside the wire."

One of the adult leaders put down the ax he was carrying and walked away, saying, "Tell him to dig it himself."

After a quiet moment, one of the teens walked over, picked up the ax, stepped across the wire, and started digging. The others shrugged, walked over with their shovels, and began refilling the previous trench, giggling and singing, "Hi-Ho, Hi-Ho!"

One hot summer afternoon in Ralls, Texas, I stood openmouthed on the front porch of my Nana's house as my cousin Ryan pulled the arms of my Stretch Armstrong doll so far that his body snapped in half and began leaking green goo all over the outdoor carpet.

I guess Ryan was born a skeptic. In any event, he sure put to test those Saturday-morning commercials claiming that one could twist and pull Mr. | *Everyone is stretched when going to another country.*

Armstrong as far as possible without "killing" the guy.

But as it turned out, even Stretch had his limits.

Likewise, you will be stretched many times during your trip. You'll have to deal with the fact that you are not in control. The language is foreign, the cultural norms are different, schedule is often of little significance, and you probably won't be in charge of where the car goes.

You will most likely be told when and where to eat, what to do, where to go . . . oh, and where to "go," too. And did I mention that the weather isn't up to you, either? Also, those "foreign noises" could keep you up at night. (I know a whole group of folks who are still recovering from their team leader's midnight concert, played entirely—and with varying instrumentation—through his nose.)

Everyone is stretched when going to another country—and sometimes just another state! When another of my many cousins, Cari, moved from mountainous Colorado to coastal California, she really didn't have to make too many adjustments. But a few years later, she moved to my old stomping ground in the flat, dry part of Texas. She basically went from an apartment overlooking the beach at Malibu to a duplex overlooking a bunch of mesquite trees.

And even though the people are generally very friendly in Texas, they were still very different from Cari. Most of her Malibu friends were what you might call "granola." They enjoyed yogurt, organic eggplant, and rock-climbing. Her new Texan friends liked black-eyed peas, corn bread, and two-stepping on Saturday night.

Now, there is nothing wrong with either; Cari simply didn't anticipate the seismic changes she found in Texas. She said she not only had to adjust to very different perspectives and people, but she also had to adjust *her own expectations*. (And if you ask me, she did rather well; she has been a full-time youth minister in Forth Worth for nearly ten years now!)

It is a difficult thing to adjust our expectations for a mission trip, but it is important to God's mission. Unrealistic expectations lead to frustration for everyone.

Many missionaries will tell you that the most significant problems arise when their own visions regarding a mission team are unrealistic. In the same way, when the team's expectations of what they are going to do, see, or accomplish are unclear or impractical, chaos ensues.

Organization, training, and preparation can prevent a lot of problems, and the experience for both your team and the people you are serving will be greatly enhanced if your expectations are modified.

> *If you are to be an effective short-termer, you must be flexible physically, mentally, and spiritually.*

The apostle James had something to say about this:

> *You ask, and don't receive, because you ask with wrong motives, so that you may spend it for your pleasures* (James 4:3, NIV).

Group training is critical, yet many missionaries have seen preparation

Anne-Geri' Fann & Greg Taylor

detract from the experience or put unrealistic expectations on the outcome. If you are to be an effective short-termer, you must be flexible physically, mentally, and spiritually.

Physical Flexibility

Don't be surprised if God decides to flex your own abilities and plans by redefining them. This could mean that you don't get to teach the sewing class you planned or host the sports camps you spent time organizing. It may mean that instead you go to the square and play soccer with the locals, or that you actually make a dress for someone who doesn't have one. *That* is physical flexibility. Now let's talk about some ways to flex those muscles . . .

1. *Volunteer according to your talents.* Everyone has something to contribute that will make the trip even more meaningful. However, as you volunteer your genius, make sure you are asking, "What is *God* trying to do?" instead of "What am *I* going to accomplish?"

2. *Implement a program that can be sustained by the residents, or work to enhance existing programs.* This kind of support to local evangelists or medical personnel helps them carry on their work. You may expect to build houses when you arrive, but find instead that there's a greater need for health classes to be taught in the schools. Perhaps you have a brilliant idea for a fund-raiser; but let the community leaders decide what the money should be used for.

3. *Deliver on what you offer.* No one wants to see the disappointment in a brother or sister's face when a promise goes unfulfilled. Do your best and offer your talents, but be realistic and work with the people in charge so that your message doesn't get lost in your promises. One female short-termer grew so attached to an orphan that she actually promised to return and take him to Disneyland! He's twenty-two years old now—I sure hope he's not still waiting.

> You've heard of the golden rule of Christ: *Do unto others as you would have them do unto you.* One of our missionary mentors, Terry Smith, suggests applying the golden rule with extreme intensity and calling it the platinum rule—one that actually fulfills Christ's intention: Do unto others as they would have you do unto them.

4. Be calm and competent. If you demonstrate that you are responsible, Christlike, calm, competent, and willing to try new things, your team leader will need you. You may find yourself in a small group where a leader is needed—and that leader could be you! However, if you prefer to stay in the background serving quietly, that is an equally admirable quality—and you will be indispensable to those leaders who need your flexible spirit and servant's heart.

5. Remember the TC Rule: Things Change! Kyle Huhtanen, a frequent missions coworker and dear friend, talks about an experiment he would like to conduct someday in order to test a mission team's mental flexibility. In his hypothetical scenario, Kyle would first schedule an ordinary trip meeting one week in advance, to be held at the church building on a Thursday night. Then, on the day of the meeting, he would reschedule the meeting to the local doughnut shop. Two hours before the meeting, it would again be rescheduled—this time for an hour later at the local park outside of town. Upon their arrival, the mission team would be drawn into a game of Duck-Duck-Goose, which would last until all present wonder why they are there and what it has to do with missions! The meeting would conclude by discussing the experiment and praying for greater flexibility during the trip.

> *God wants you to be teachable. If you reach a point where you know everything, you have stopped growing in Christ.*

The lesson: God wants you to be teachable. If you reach a point where you know everything, you have stopped growing in Christ.

Mental Flexibility

Everyone has, at one point or another, seen things from a limited perspective. Maybe your teacher was having a bad week but you thought she had it out for you. Perhaps your mom made you practice the piano every day when you were young, and you thought she was just being mean.

Once, when asked at a Sonic drive-in, "Would you like fries with that?" I responded in irritation, "Did I *ask* for fries with that?" (Yeah, I'm not proud of this.)

I immediately felt horrible about my knee-jerk response and went inside to apologize. I discovered that the employees were instructed to repeat that line to every customer. I also found out that the person working the drive-thru was physically impaired and having a difficult enough time just doing his job (did I mention I'm not proud of this?).

The more we try to look at things from others' perspectives, the better we will understand their lifestyle and what is important to them. *That* is mental flexibility.

Here are some examples:

1. Remember that being different doesn't mean you're better than them. The following story is a classic example of operating under the assumption that there is no civilization outside the U.S.

Molly Dawidow, a missionary in Poland, had a somewhat naive woman come help them with her work. One day the woman came into the office just as Molly was on her

 Culture is like a pair of glasses. . . . when you try on someone else's lenses, things become freakishly blurry!

way out to a doctor's appointment. She asked if Molly was sick.

"No," Molly replied, "I'm just going for my annual checkup with the gynecologist."

The woman's eyes grew enormous, and she asked in astonishment, "They have gynecologists in Poland?"

Molly countered by joking, "No, of course not! Polish women don't have reproductive organs—the storks bring the babies!"

2. Ask questions. Inquiry is one of the best ways to find out more about people. Remember, however, to ask questions with *service* and *learning* in mind. "Why do they do it that way?" can too easily be interpreted as, "My way is better." "Why are we going there?" can be taken to mean, "You must not know what you're doing."

Instead, try saying, "This is pretty different from what I'm used to; could you explain it to me?" Or frame your question with enthusiasm: "What are we going to do today?"

3. Put on some new glasses. Culture, like your own pair of glasses, helps you see things clearly but from a fairly limited perspective. When you try on someone else's lenses, things become freakishly blurry!

However, an interesting thing happens: The longer you wear the new pair, the harder your eyes work to adjust. In the same way, the harder you try to look at things from others' perspectives, the more you will begin to understand them, their lifestyle, and what is important to them.

4. Eat lunch in someone's home. This may be a challenge if you have decided to go on a mission trip in a country that serves unfamiliar food. But eating at another's table makes a world of difference to those people who are serving you their culinary delights. Get over your food hang-ups, refrain from making faces, and graciously accept their hospitality. The kids I've seen make an effort in these situations remember little afterward but the blessing of the experience.

Now, people generally understand if you have health-related dietary needs (diabetes, for example). But just remember the girl who decided it was okay not to be a vegetarian for a meal, the guy who realized his strict diet would offend his hosts and quickly "got over it," and the senior leader who, although trying to cut out caffeine, still maintains that it was the only time in his life coffee actually put him to sleep! He looked at it as God's little blessing on his decision to cultivate a relationship instead of refusing a hot cup of brew.

And now, a sensitive topic. In some countries, alcohol may be served along with a meal. These drinks are generally not strong and sometimes even watered down, such as wine. What do you do? Should you drink it?

If a strange drink is placed before you or you know it is alcoholic, you could ask your leader what to do. Will it hurt to sip the drink? If you are under age for drinking in the U.S., you have a very good reason not to drink. You can be matter-of-fact about this without offending your hosts.

Be prepared: In many countries, wine is used in the Eucharist or Lord's Supper. If you've never had wine before, it may sting your lips.

The concepts of mental flexibility were first introduced to me years ago in Harper Lee's To Kill a Mockingbird. *Atticus Finch, the noble lawyer from Maycomb, Alabama, tells his daughter that the simple trick for getting along with all kinds of folks is to consider things from their point of view. After the trial of Tom Robinson, a black man who was found guilty for a crime everyone knew he didn't commit, Finch revisits the concept: "You never really understand a person until you consider things from his point of view . . . until you climb into his skin and walk around in it."*

You should discuss this possibility with your leader before the trip and plan in advance what you will do. Above all, do not attempt to preach the "evils" of drinking alcohol to the nationals. They may drink wine with every meal but never get drunk.

On the opposite end of the spectrum, we've seen short-termers offered local brew in African villages by "the beer club"—the equivalent of the local bar—and we encourage them *not* to drink then. The Christians in that particular village believed that part of their discipleship in Christ was to completely abstain from alcohol; they used fruit juice for the Lord's Supper. (Many short-termers and their parents ask more questions about food than any other topic. We've written more about eating on page 21.)

Spiritual Flexibility

In addition to mental and physical flexibility, you will also need spiritual flexibility on your short-term mission trip. Think seriously about the following spiritual principles.

1. It's not about me. Remind yourself again and again that the trip is not about you. Recharge your spirit by remembering and reviewing the purpose of God: to redeem and restore a good relationship with His children in every corner of the globe.

> *As missionary Steve Meeks says, "Our church is not the message. Our country is not the message. Good hygiene, education, financial stewardship, better planting methods, baptism, the Holy Spirit, and heaven are not the message. Jesus, as representative of the nature of God and as the Savior of the world, is the message. Jesus Himself said, 'I am the way, the truth, and the life.' It was His way of simply laying out what message we should bring to the world."*

We are human and therefore prone to exhaustion and frustration. It is okay to grow tired or feel underutilized. But remember first that this trip is about Jesus.

2. Have a settled attitude of soul. When Mary and Martha lost their beloved brother, Lazarus, they were distraught that Jesus was not around to do something about it. But Jesus, who is master over time and space, raised Lazarus and renewed Martha's faith: "I believe that you are the Christ" (John 11:27 NIV).

Like Martha, you can begin your trip with a settled soul and the belief that only Christ can prepare you for what you are about to experience; only Jesus can raise you up.

While on the trip, recharge your "personal batteries" with the same thought: *My true mission is about Jesus.*

Anything can happen on your trip. There can be joy, compassion, and real understanding of service. There can also be annoyances, hang-ups, and conflicts. The occasional trip will involve an accident or a tragedy, perhaps even a death. But even Lazarus died again; he did not stay alive forever, and neither will we. Whatever happens, the trip is about Jesus.

3. *Imagine yourself in the middle of a marathon, not a sprint.* You never know how your service to someone is going to affect their understanding of God and His kingdom. The children you taught in Thailand may not remember you five years later, but they'll remember that a special, "different" person came to their school and taught them to love God. To accomplish something is a good feeling, but it's good to remember that there is more to be done.

Jesus Flexes His Muscles

Jesus was the ultimate "Stretch Armstrong"—an incredible example of flexibility. Let's take a closer look at the temptations He faced during His forty-day fast.

1. Jesus was challenged physically.

> *The devil said to him, "If you are the Son of God, tell this stone to become bread." Jesus answered, "It is written: 'Man does not live on bread alone.'"* (Luke 4:3–4 NIV)

> *Remember, you can do a lot more for people when you understand them, not just feed them.*

Jesus was called to feed Himself through miraculous means, something the Jewish people would have loved because it was the kind of thing they expected to see from their Messiah. But it would have taken Jesus out of the human experience—we wouldn't be able to say He suffered as we do.

Have you ever been truly hungry? If you should find yourself in a situation where you must go many hours without food—or at least, food that you like!—remember what Jesus went through to understand us, to experience true hunger.

On this trip you may see children who eat only one meal a day and feel called to suffer along with them. Perhaps you will experience your first pangs of true hunger.

2. Jesus was challenged spiritually.

> *The devil led him up to a high place and showed him in an instant all the kingdoms of the world. And he said to him, "I will give you all their authority and splendor, for it has been*

given to me, and I can give it to anyone I want to. So if you worship me, it will all be yours." Jesus answered, "It is written: 'Worship the Lord your God and serve him only.'" (Luke 4:5–8 NIV)

Satan's control was limited on this occasion, so why was it a temptation? I would venture to guess that if Jesus accepted the kingdoms of the world, His job was finished! It may have prevented His suffering, but trust and free will would have gone out the window.

Remember, just because your trip is short-term, cutting corners is no way to save souls. What does this mean? It means that making promises you can't keep or handing out money does not necessarily help people. Consider how you would feel if someone showed up in your neighborhood and offered to "solve" all your problems—then left town after a week.

The best thing you can do is pray with them, learn from them, understand them, suffer with them, and enjoy time together.

3. Jesus was challenged mentally.

The devil led him to Jerusalem and had him stand on the highest point of the temple. "If you are the Son of God," he said, "throw yourself down from here. For it is written: '"He will command his angels concerning you to guard you carefully; they will lift you up in their hands, so that you will not strike your foot against a stone."'" Jesus answered, "It says: 'Do not put the Lord your God to the test.'" (Luke 4:9–12 NIV)

Satan took Jesus to the "highest point," the apex of the sanctuary, the top of

---

Jesus Knew What to Expect

To Nicodemus, a ruler who sought Him out, Jesus said, "Unless one is born of water . . ." To the Samaritan woman, an outcast whom Jesus sought out, He said, "Whoever drinks of this living water will never thirst."

In both instances Jesus used water to explain what life is all about. In one sense, the water springs up from a different well to eternal life. In another, it is flowing through the birth canal with the Spirit to enter into eternal life in the kingdom of God. In each case, Jesus offers something new by comparing it to something they could understand—water.

He knew exactly where each was coming from, and to what extent both would listen. He knew what Nicodemus was fishing for and therefore what bait would hook his intellect. He knew that the woman wasn't necessarily searching, but that she needed to be searched—needed someone to reach into the deep well of her soul and draw forth honesty and conviction.

Jesus did not assume what to expect; He knew. This attitude is potable "water." This is the kind of water you need to pour into your canteen and pack along on your mission trip.

Solomon's porch, also called the royal portico. Then the deceiver told Jesus to toss Himself down and wait for angels. Now, this risky leap would have saved a lot of time, but His message would have been misunderstood and God's plans thwarted.

You may think you can do things better than the locals or even the missionaries in the host country. Are you being tempted by the deceiver to believe you are powerful?

Perhaps you will stand on a hill overlooking a city with millions of people. In that moment, do you pray for God to act or do you feel you can change things yourself?

Flexibility, Green Goo, God, and You

Stretch Armstrong didn't see it coming that hot summer day Ryan ended his plastic life. But ironically, that toy taught my cousin a valuable lesson.

Remember the TC rule? *Things change!* That is now Ryan's catchy mantra. And he's no longer bludgeoning inanimate action figures. In fact, he and his wife are full-time missionaries in Mexico City. He says, "Planning is good and necessary, but don't expect things to go exactly as planned."

God's true mission through your journey is all about bringing Christ along with the bag of rice, about coming to know Him and His people. It is not about whether a trench was wisely dug around someone's house, but rather about your willingness to dig and the community you create with those you serve.

You cannot share Christ unless you become like Him. And you also cannot share Him unless you become somewhat like those you are sharing Him with.

ETERNAL ENDEAVORS____

The following activities will help you see things from another perspective, practice your flexibility, get prepared for the next chapter, and make you laugh out loud. (Solutions follow.)

Activities

1. Puzzlement
• Have a parent or friend buy an inexpensive child's puzzle—something containing between ten and twenty pieces.
• Without letting you see the box top, have a parent or friend hide the puzzle pieces in various places in your house.
• Set a stopwatch for three minutes.
• When your parent/friend says, "Go!" run around the house finding the pieces as quickly as possible. Try to find them all and then assemble the puzzle in less than three minutes.
• Can't do it? That's okay. Next read the solution in the section that follows. (And don't cheat! Read it *last*.)

2. I hope you're not allergic to rubber bands
Wear a rubber band around your wrist during the mission trip to remind you to remain calm and flexible in all situations.

My husband's last engineering team to Honduras wore some "Never Give Up" wristbands from the ALS Association for Lou Gehrig's Disease. You can find inexpensive ones (that won't snag your arm hairs) in many different stores.

Wear it to remember to be flexible. If you're bold, give it a little snap whenever you realize you weren't particularly calm or flexible (oh, you'll know).

3. Wholly paper
Get three other friends to do this activity with you.

Three of you should each take a blank piece of paper. Have the fourth person read aloud the instructions below, waiting until each task is finished. *(Do not change these directions in any way, because it won't work!)*

1. "Close your eyes." (Make sure everyone is doing this!)
2. "Take the paper and fold it in half."
3. "Tear the top left corner of the paper."
4. "Now turn the paper upside down."

---

5. "Tear the top right corner of the paper."
6. "Fold the paper in half again."
7. "Now tear the bottom right corner of the paper."
8. "Fold the paper in half one more time."
9. "Tear the bottom left corner of the paper."
10. "Open your eyes."

Now look at your papers. Are they exactly the same? Highly doubtful. Why?

Solutions

1. Puzzlement

As you will learn in the next chapter, there are many pieces to the cultural puzzle. You can't compare another culture to your own, and you won't have the "box top" to understand what big picture you are trying to put together! *Be flexible.* Don't assume you know what something looks like just because you have figured out a few "pieces" to the cultural puzzle.

2. I hope you're not allergic to rubber bands

This one is a reminder to remain calm and flexible in all situations. *May you have unmarked wrists at the end of your trip!*

3. Wholly paper

No one is going to listen to instructions the exact same way when their eyes are closed. Everyone's perspective of "right corner" and "left bottom" is different when we don't understand the starting point. Flexibility will add to your patience in another culture.

FOOD

Eating meals in the homes of people in your target location may be the most important thing you do to show them love. And it may be the most important thing you do to *receive* their love.

Imagine with me for a minute. For the last year, you've saved Christmas money, birthday money, and your allowance so that you can spend it on a feast for a group of visiting foreign exchange students. You even scrub the toilets, ironed the tablecloth, and polished the silver forks in anticipation. For two days, you work in your kitchen cooking your favorite family recipes handed down through generations. In the hours before their arrival, you put on your finest clothes and make sure everything was "just right." Your stomach ties itself in knots. You can hear your pulse in your ears.

Then, the car pulls up outside. Three strangely-dressed people climb out with their guide and make their way up the front walk. You quickly notice that they spoke no English. *Oh well,* you reason to yourself, *they're from a foreign country.*

You lead them around your home on a tour. All the while, the two young ladies in the group whisper to each other and point. A few times, they even giggle. The young man looks bored.

You end your tour in the dining room where you usher each guest to his or her chair. The moment has arrived. You serve your lovingly prepared meal, but your guests just pick at their food. The guide translates and everyone makes polite conversation. Near the end of the meal, the young man pulls out a baggie full of cheese and crackers. He tries to eat them without you noticing, but you do anyway.

Your guest leave and you return to the dining room. All that work. All that anticipation. You begin to clean up by picking up a napkin. Out spills two or three bites of your favorite dish. *She spit it out!*

How do you feel?

Imagine how it would feel to someone who sacrifices from their meager financial means to feed you and you bring your own peanut butter and crackers, barely touch what they offer, or turn up your nose.

During His time on earth, Jesus ministered at the table. We do what Jesus did, including eating food we may not like. Can you picture Jesus turning His nose up at food served to Him? Or do you picture Jesus graciously accepting food from humble servants in homes throughout Judea and Samaria?

You may not think you are doing something offensive by making a face, whispering to your friend, making eyes across the table, or laughing loudly, but these are cues that anyone can pick up in any language!

You may only have one or two opportunities to sit at someone's table. Realize that local people anticipate this for months. They are usually scraping together money and food to prepare a meal for their first-ever international visitors. Typically, they want to please you. They are excited about their visitors. They will be extremely disappointed if they don't get to talk with you, share food with you. They would be crushed if they thought you didn't like their food.

Greg sat in the shade of a mango tree with three men in Bulanga village, full to his larynx with spinach and cornmeal mush. The men knew he'd just eaten at another home in Bulanga. But they feed him again—spinach and cornmeal mush. They feed him because it's important that Greg eat together with them at their table. Then, they fed him a course of white sweet potatoes dipped in soup of tomatoes, onions, and oil. The table is not just where friendships are made. The table *is* friendship.

The meal wasn't complete without another course—termites in a bowl. They were still alive! It was only a joke to spook the missionary. The men, still laughing, took the termites back, sautéed them, and added salt to make a nice afternoon snack. Greg saved most for the children in the village. They ate them by the handful with smiles on their faces.

In Uganda, the food "belongs" to the visitor. The visitor who graciously shares his food with the children is generous. For example, a family may only be able to afford to serve chicken six times a year. The family is thrilled to serve a feast and give the visitor generous portions. The children are very happy to see some meat return to them.

What part of the chicken is prized and saved for the guest? The gizzard. Do you know what the gizzard is? It's part of a chicken's digestive system! Greg ate many gizzards in his years in Uganda!

You may need to eat more strange food than you want to. But by doing so, you will show love to your hosts and accept love from them!

Christ's Example

What if you could sit and learn missionary table etiquette from Jesus? Look at the Gospel of Luke and you'll find nearly a dozen examples of Jesus as gracious guest and host of a table meal.

Jesus went to a party thrown by a tax man. Tax collectors were the con men of His day bilking Jews for more money than they really owed the Roman government. The religious leaders complained. They couldn't understand why Jesus would eat with the scum of the earth. Jesus demonstrated that sharing the gospel is more important than keeping the customs and rules of a cultural group. He said, and I paraphrase, "A good doctor doesn't spend the bulk of his time with well people, but the sick" (Luke 5:27–32).

Jesus also ate with people from His own culture, the Jews. During the meal, servants were likely coming in and out of the room bringing food. Somehow, a prostitute slipped in and began pouring perfume on Jesus's feet. The self-righteous host was indignant. He wondered aloud how a prophet could allow an obviously sinful woman to caress His feet. Jesus did not refuse her hospitality. He forgave her sins. The people watching were amazed and wondered who this man was who could forgive sins (Luke 7:37–50).

You've heard the story of Jesus feeding the five thousand. Jesus hosts the meal and instructs His disciples to feed others as well. If someone is feeding you, they too are fulfilling a mission Jesus gave His disciples: "give them something to eat" (Luke 9:10–17).

When Jesus sent out the seventy disciples, he told them to "eat what is set before you" (Luke 10:8). The apostle Paul also exhorts Christians to eat food without questions when they are fellowshipping with others (1 Cor 8:4–8).

If Jesus believes sharing meals with others is part of His mission, don't you think we ought to take the dinner table seriously? (For more illustrations of Jesus accepting or giving hospitality, see Luke 10:38–42; 11:37–54; 14:1–24; 19:1–10; 24:30–35, 45–49.)

A Soga proverb says, "Friends eat together." The table means friendship. No friendship in Soga gets very far without shared meals. A Ugandan friend of Greg's—between bites of sweet potato—told him, "We enjoy your Bible studies, Taylor, but we want you to sit, eat, and talk with us more, like you are doing now." Greg promised Patrick not to preach less, but to sit at his table more.

What Happens at Your Table?
In Ugandan homes, the most important piece of furniture is the table.

The table also means redemption. In Soga culture, if a son brings shame to his father, eating a meal at the same table is how the father communicates forgiveness to his son.

The table is also the most important piece of furniture in our churches. The communion table is redemption. Around His table, our Heavenly Father continues to communicate forgiveness to us. Jesus, our host, says, "Greater love has no one than this, that he lay down his life for his friends. Do this to remember Me, My friends."

What's your table for?

As my friend John Mark Hicks says,

> The table is a place where Jesus was both a gracious guest and gracious host. So the table is a place where the church welcomes strangers (aliens). The table has a missionary quality, especially in light of the fact that the disciples receive their call to missions at a table. The table

is a place where Jesus receives sinners and confronts the righteous. The table is the place where Jesus extends grace to seekers, but condemns the self-righteous. Jesus is willing to eat with sinners in order to invite them into the kingdom . . . The last (sinners, poor, and humbled) will be first in the kingdom of God, but the first (self-righteous, rich, and proud) will be last and excluded from the kingdom of God (Luke 13:26–30).[1]

Here's the Kicker

Eating together with God's children in another country is one of the God-given and Jesus-modeled ways to be the body of Christ. Sharing a meal graciously and lovingly is a way to team up with Christ in the way He does business.

[1]"The Missional Table," *Wineskins Magazine,* www.wineskins.org, Sep/Oct 2002.

ENTERING A FOREIGN CULTURE

3

Missionary Moment ...

During a mission to Africa, some North American visitors witnessed an old woman in the street shaking hands with a very young boy and calling him "grandfather." A few of the short-termers assumed she was some kind of nutter, some thought she was blind and couldn't see the poor kid, and others thought it was just a joke. But the reality is that this sweet old woman really thought the kiddo was her grandfather.

What the visitors in the above example witnessed was a glimpse into another culture they didn't fully comprehend. Read on as a step toward understanding.

Some dog owners install an invisible fence to keep their puppies within bounds. When they try to cross the boundary, they get a tiny electric zap, a little reminder that they have traipsed into the forbidden zone. Most dogs adapt well and stay within their boundaries. After all, who wants to get zapped? Pups don't typically need to be told twice.

So, too, the invisible fences in cross-cultural communication can often zap a first-time missionary enough that he or she may not particularly want to venture out again.

In order to prepare for a foreign culture, it may help to think about the admittedly far-fetched example of first contact with

> *The invisible fences in cross-cultural communication can often zap a first-time missionary enough that he or she may not particularly want to venture out again.*

aliens by considering what their first impression of us would be like. Science fiction literature and sci-fi flicks offer a hefty commentary on current events and the social climate through a broad range of theories: There is the "oh-no-they're-coming-we're-all-gonna-die" reaction, as in H. G. Wells's *War of the Worlds;* or the "aliens-love-us-and-are-really-only-stuck-on-our-planet" premise, as seen in Stephen Spielberg's E. T.

What kind of impression do Americans generally make on other cultures? History shows we:

a. kill them,

b. enslave them,

c. assimilate them, or

d. convert them to our religion.

Funny that history never reveals a time where we actually left people alone!

The concept of the Prime Directive from *Star Trek* essentially states, "You will not intervene in the natural order of other life forms." This concept suggests that in the future we will have learned from past mistakes through first contact with other cultures and created rules to govern such encounters.[4]

But how does this apply to mission work? Let's find out.

1. What Is Culture, Anyway?

According to the dictionary, culture is defined as "the customary beliefs, social forms, and material traits of a racial, religious, or social group." It affects who we are as individuals and molds us as societies. Our culture is the foundation for our worldview, how we perceive reality. *It shapes who we are.*

We sometimes look at events in other cultures and make assumptions or judgments based upon our own experiences. As a result of not understanding the

 Culture is like the air we breathe: taken for granted, but impossible to live without.

culture, our assumptions are often incorrect. The worldview for someone in Thailand is going to be different from the worldview of someone in Texas.

Study the chart on page 27. Notice that behaviors are on the outside—the skin of the apple. The values, like the fruit's flesh, lie beneath the skin and contribute to visible behaviors. At the core is what makes us grow and tick and think: our worldview.[5]

Remember in this chapter's Missionary Moment the Kipsigis grandmother who called a seven-year-old child her "grandfather"? Here's the background on that scene.

When a child is born, her people perform the Kurenet rite ("the calling"). The women call out ancestral names ("Are you Arap Tonui?") until the child sneezes. This group firmly believes that the child is the spirit and name of the ancestor that lives in the person of the new baby. "Hello, grandfather" was not the muttering of a crazy woman, but an actual family greeting.[6]

This is an example of a *behavior* that stems from a *value* (respect for ancestors), which is grounded in an animistic *worldview* (life is a cycle and those who "came before" are part of it). The verse "In the beginning, God created the heavens and the earth" may be understood differently by those of us with a "beginning and

Anne-Geri' Fann & Greg Taylor

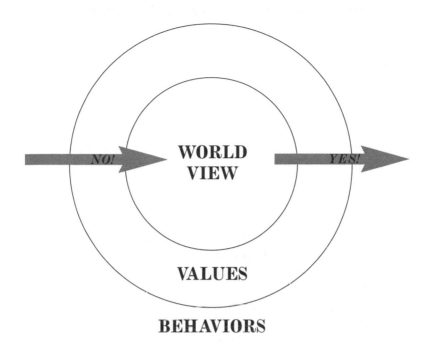

WORLD
VIEW

NO! → ← *YES!*

VALUES

BEHAVIORS

end" view of time, but it's is not going to carry a lot of weight with the Kipsigis.

Through this example, you can see that if any missionary (short- or long-term) looks closely at another's worldview, the gospel will become much more relevant to that person and the missionary will have a successful experience. In other words, if you examine the culture you are visiting without assuming your

 Language is more than just the words coming out of someone's mouth.

own is superior, you take a big step toward identification—which is at the heart of the Christian faith.

2. Why Is Culture Important?

"The Word became flesh, and dwelt among us." (John 1:14 NASB)

The Incarnation is the most amazing mystery of our faith. God, the "eternal, immortal, invisible," put on the robe of humanity and became like us. Missionary Herbert Kane said that so complete and perfect was God's identification with us that one must look a second time to discover His divinity.[7]

This truth of the incarnation of Jesus as a human is why *identifying with the people* should be your primary objective. Obviously, this challenge will prove more difficult in some cultures than others; but it is the attitude and spirit of

---

the attempt that goes a long way with the people and opens hearts to the message you're there to share.

In my Spanish language classes, I always have a message posted on my wall or website that reads, "Learn a language, speak a culture." Relay your message in a way that makes sense to your audience.

You see, language is more than just the words coming out of someone's mouth. A missionary will discover it in gestures, in the meaning behind songs, in the stories of the people, and in many other behaviors. The fun part of learning a language (and this is true even if your "target mission" is your hometown!) is gaining an understanding of those symbols and traditions; it is putting *yourself* "into context" by relating to another culture, or even the one you already live in.

It's important to remember that different cultures perceive "reality" in completely different ways. Even the most awkward attempts to understand an unknown culture can teach you a good deal about how change happens.

Remember, *become a learner first and a teacher second.*

3. How Is Culture Relevant to My Trip?

The average North American, instead of being a learner first, "lumps all groups together and proceeds without references to basic *cultural* differences."[8] Truth be known, many short-termers are guilty of this. It is an easy offense to commit when one is in a place for a short period of time and doing his or her best to make a difference.

It is unfair to judge another culture by Western standards or even modern interpretations of Scripture. North America is *not* singularly blessed with divine guidance. All nations stand equal under the sovereignty of God, and we must assume that God is working through other cultural heritages as well.

Paul's aim was to be relevant so that the gospel would be relevant, and he strove to become like those he was trying to reach. Thus, the way he preached in the synagogue in Pisidian Antioch was different from how he preached in the Areopagus in Athens. While his *message* was always the same—"Jesus Christ and Him crucified"—his *methods* varied to fit the context.

Being aware will go a long way in a different culture, so listen and learn. Now, I'm *not* saying that anything is excusable so long as its basis is derived from another culture. Clearly, this is untrue. There are things about our own culture that are inherently sinful—I'm sure you can think of many examples. What I'm saying is that you can share the truth only when you *learn before you teach.* Otherwise, you will sabotage your own good motives.

How is all of this relevant to your trip? Well, look at the Lord's words through Paul: *to bring good news to the poor, the sinners, the weak.* At the heart of the Christian faith is *love of our neighbors* and *sharing our hope with them.*

Do not consider yourself a missionary just yet; rather, see yourself as a missionary in training. Study the successful ones on the field—observe how they react to the culture and identify with the people. Most important, look at their relationships with God.

God created culture; Satan is the one who bent it all out of shape. But then Jesus came to earth for us, working *through* culture. His primary goals were to save us, redeem us, and restore our relationship with God.

Understanding culture (including your own), finding ways to filter your experiences within that culture, and realizing your place in the context of mission work are all valuable tools to prevent being zapped by the invisible fence of culture.

ETERNAL ENDEAVORS

Let's have a little bit of fun with a quiz. Read each of the following scenarios and choose the answer that best fits what you would do in a similar situation. (Note: Some of these are made up and others are drawn from real-life mission experiences.) Remember that although you may think of a fourth or fifth option, these possibilities are based on past statements made by short-termers.

A discussion of each scenario follows. Have fun!

Quiz

1. Grandma Speaks to Ghosts

Let's pretend you were the short-termer who saw the old woman calling the young boy "grandfather" in the Missionary Moment at the beginning of the chapter. There is a big difference between how a culturally aware person and an unprepared person might react to this scene. How would you most likely respond?

    a. "Did you hear that? I'll bet she's slow or maybe crazy."

    b. "How interesting! I wonder why she's calling him 'grandfather'?"

    c. No response.

2. Responding to Haitian Hardships

You have just returned from a trip to Haiti, where you witnessed great poverty. But you also saw a simpler way of life than what you are used to. Here are some possible responses:

    a. "I want to move back there and be a missionary."

    b. "They're happy with so little. I want to be more like that."

    c. "I'll continue to pray for God to show me more about these people and my place in His work in their country."

3. German Jargon

You are on lunch break at a mission church in Hanover, Germany. Your team leader and a church member sit at your table. The church member looks at you, then at the team leader, and says, *"Daran wird jedermann erkennen, daß ihr meine Jünger seid, wenn ihr Liebe untereinander habt."* They exchange a good-natured laugh, but you have no idea what was said. You think to yourself,

    a. I should ask what they are saying. It sounds like they are enjoying themselves.

    b. They must be laughing at me.

    c. I don't mean to be rude, but I kind of think people should speak my language if they are with me and I don't speak theirs. I am trying to relate to other cultures; isn't it fair that they try to relate to me?

4. Jesus Versus Judas

Don Richardson was a missionary to New Guinea in the seventies. He spent years working with a tribe of former cannibals who were not very far removed from their former way of life. Mr. Richardson had a very difficult time teaching the gospel of Jesus to this group because they would lift up Judas as a hero every time he got to that part in the story. What advice would you give Mr. Richardson?

a. "Keep telling the story. The gospel message is the same everywhere. Eventually someone will understand. If not, maybe you should leave. The Bible does say to 'shake the dust off your feet' if they don't accept the message!"

b. "There has to be some reason they like Judas. Find out more about who they are as a people before you continue with the message. There may be something you are missing."

c. "Hold a seminar on how to study the Bible."

5. Steel Axes for Stone-Age Australians

You are a short-term missionary to the Yir Yiront, an aboriginal people in Australia who are still considered to be living in the Stone Age. You notice that the whole tribe is using the same stone ax and passing back and forth. This makes work go very slowly, especially since the ax has to be returned each day to one man who is its keeper. You are trying to find a way to help them. What do you do?

a. Do nothing but serve and minister to the people.

b. Show them how to make steel axes for every family so that work can get done more quickly and their lives can ultimately improve.

c. Go home and tell people how fortunate they are to live in a society that is not so primitive.

6. Misunderstood in Mexico

It is your fifth year visiting a children's home in Mexico. You have been going since tenth grade with your youth group and have continued through college. You have developed relationships with the children and watched some of them enter high school. You have a good relationship with the administration. You are about to graduate from college with a degree in social work, and you would

ETERNAL ENDEAVORS

like to move to the children's home to work as a missionary. You put in an application, but it is kindly refused. What are your options?

    a. It is okay to be a little angry. You devoted years to this project and are highly qualified to do the work there.

    b. Look for work elsewhere. This may not be the right time. Put in an application next year.

    c. Continue to communicate with the children's home and try to spend more than a week there at a time. Keep your eyes open for other ways you can serve.

7. Communicating with Cannibals

You are with a group of short-termers who are sharing the concept of the Lord's Supper to a group of formerly cannibalistic Maoris on the island of Fiji. However, the verse "Whoever eats my flesh and drinks my blood" does not communicate the message for which you are hoping. What should you do?

    a. Laugh a little. You've got to admit, it is pretty funny.

    b. Retell the communion story in your own words.

    c. Serve something different, like Coca-cola and tortilla chips.

8. To Kneel or Not to Kneel?

You are in southeastern Uganda, where traditional Basoga women and children kneel when they greet others. You see women kneeling before men and other women that approach her on a path, and you witness another women kneeling in church—this time to greet *you*! What should you do?

    a. Tell the woman to get up; she shouldn't bow to you. Didn't Paul and Barnabas tell the crowds in Lystra not to bow down to them?

    b. Chastise the men for the way they've forced women to kneel when they greet. Question why the men don't also do it.

    c. Ask one of the local people about the tradition of kneeling, its origin, and what it means.

Discussion Guide

So how do you think you did?

1. Grandma Speaks to Ghosts

The possible answers were:

    a. "Did you hear that? I'll bet she's slow or maybe crazy."

    b. "How interesting! I wonder why is she calling him 'grandfather'?"

    c. No response.

Clearly, response "a" would be a choice made in ignorance. Not necessarily stupidity, just not-getting-it ignorance. But according to the case study, somebody actually said it. Some may opt for "c." This is not a rude reaction, but if one's eyes are purposefully open and seeking to be a learner, a response would almost be expected! **"B" is the best answer** and will get you a long way in your relationship and communication with the people you are trying to reach.

2. Responding to Haitian Hardships

The possible answers were:

    a. "I want to move back there and be a missionary."

    b. "They're happy with so little. I want to be more like that."

    c. "I'll continue to pray for God to show me more about these people and my place in His work in their country."

It is a noble idea, but "a" is impulsive. No one should make a decision based on such a brief encounter—yet many people have! "B" is, again, a little ignorant (in the nicest sense of the word). Sorry, folks, but it's not true. The sad truth is that many in impoverished countries typically have an underlying fatalistic attitude. It should come as no surprise that many of these people have come illegally to countries they consider affluent. **"C" is the best answer** because it shows you are listening to God and seeking your place in working to bring souls to Him.

3. German Jargon

The possible answers were:

    a. I should ask what they are saying. It sounds like they are enjoying themselves.

    b. They must be laughing at me.

c. I don't mean to be rude, but I kind of think people should speak my language if they are with me and I don't speak theirs. I am trying to relate to other cultures; isn't it fair that they try to relate to me?

Many people can relate to the frustration of not understanding a language or feeling like someone is talking about you. But the German sentence was actually a recitation of John 13:35—"By this all men will know that you are my disciples, if you love one another." The German church member *was* referring to you—and it was a compliment to your time and work in his country. **The best answer is "a."**

4. Jesus Versus Judas
The possible answers were:
  a. "Keep telling the story. The gospel message is the same everywhere. Eventually someone will understand. If not, maybe you should leave. The Bible does say to 'shake the dust off your feet' if they don't accept the message!"
  b. "There has to be some reason they like Judas. Find out more about who they are as a people before you continue with the message. There may be something you are missing."
  c. "Hold a seminar on how to study the Bible."

As you may have guessed, this is a true story. Treachery was a way of life to the Sawi of New Guinea. When they were cannibals, it was a great honor to have "fattened someone with friendship for the slaughter."[9] They would befriend them, invite them into their homes, and then "have them for dinner"—literally. You can't call Judas "the bad guy" in a culture of self-described deceivers.

The "gospel" is not the same everywhere. In the real story, the only way this tribe finally understood Jesus was for Mr. Richardson to watch and listen long enough to finally observe some things. You see, the rivaling tribes would often trade their leaders' firstborn to live among the families of the other tribe and be raised by the other chief's family and the community. As long as that "peace child" was alive, there was peace between the tribes.

When Mr. Richardson introduced Jesus as the Peace Child for a world at war against the spiritual forces of darkness, they understood. **The best answer is "b."**

5. Steel Axes for Stone-Age Australians

The possible answers were:

a. Do nothing but serve and minister to the people.

b. Show them how to make steel axes for every family so that work can get done more quickly and their lives can ultimately improve.

c. Go home and tell people how fortunate they are to live in a society that is not so primitive.

In Lauriston Sharp's article "Steel Axes for Stone-Age Australians," the Yir Yiront of Australia were said to still be living in the "Stone Age."

This people group eventually broke apart when missionaries brought in steel axes for every family. Why? Because it was the patriarch of the family who held the stone ax; it was a significant representation of masculinity. The ax was the property of the adult males, and everyone in the class structure accepted this. Women and children could use the ax if they asked, but none of them actually owned one. The advent of the steel axes wrought separation: Without one leader, there was no tribe.[10]

It is important to learn how a culture operates before new ideas about God are introduced. Although the culture may be considered "primitive" by our standards, it is still a developing place. We can learn a lot from that. **The best answer is "a."**

6. Misunderstood in Mexico

These were the possible answers:

a. It is okay to be a little angry. You devoted years to this project and are highly qualified to do the work there.

b. Look for work elsewhere. This may not be the right time. Put in an application next year.

c. Continue to communicate with the children's home and try to spend more than a week there at a time. Keep your eyes open for other ways you can serve.

One reason the City of Children in Ensenada, Mexico, refuses to hire anyone but Mexicans *from that area* is because they have been "burned" by good-hearted people who have chosen to judge the project by North American standards. The problems this has caused have reinforced their need for national workers.

Regardless of how ready you are to serve, it is imperative that you also respect the experience of others and understand that there may be a reason for the rejection. Their policies may change. Also, the more time you spend there, the more likely it is that you will be considered, regardless of your nationality, because they *know* you. **The best answer is "c."**

7. Communicating with Cannibals
The possible answers were:
   a. Laugh a little. You've got to admit, it is pretty funny.
   b. Retell the communion story in your own words.
   c. Serve something different, like Coca-cola and tortilla chips.

As irreligious as it may seem, **the best answer is "b."** And although the last answer has applied in other mission situations, we would do well to take the advice of Don Richardson from Number 4 and find a way to communicate the same message in a different manner. Can you think of some ways to do this?

8. To Kneel or Not to Kneel?
The possible answers were:
   a. Tell the woman to get up; she shouldn't bow to you. Didn't Paul and Barnabas tell the crowds in Lystra not to bow down to them?
   b. Chastise the men for the way they've forced women to kneel when they greet. Question why the men don't also do it.
   c. Ask one of the local people about the tradition of kneeling, its origin, and what it means.

We have witnessed short-termers actually ask a woman to get up, but this only served to confuse her. Answer "a" assumes (falsely) that you understand what a woman or child is communicating by kneeling.

The second response is not likely to be well received, either—particularly if you do not understand why the person is kneeling in the first place.

The background on this scenario is that the Basoga women of Uganda kneel in the presence of both men and women. The tradition is not so much wrapped up in female servitude to men as it is a show of respect to leaders, both male and female.

In our work in Africa, we've seen women kneel before other respected women, aunts, and grandmothers. Parents teach their children to kneel as a way of respect, in much the same way that parents in the United States teach their children to say, "Yes, ma'am," or "No, sir."

Anne-Geri' Fann & Greg Taylor

The best answer is "c." Discover the ways other cultures show respect, honor, or dishonor. Granted, some people abuse the respect of others—acknowledging the good of a cultural tradition does not always negate the possibility of misuse.

WHAT YOU HAVE TO OFFER

4

Missionary Moment ...

From a *Time* magazine interview with Mother Teresa:

> **Journalist:** *Humble as you are, it must be an extraordinary thing to be a vehicle of God's grace in the world.*
>
> **Mother Teresa:** *But it is His work. I think God wants to show His greatness by using nothingness.*
>
> **Journalist:** *You feel you have no special qualities?*
>
> **Mother Teresa:** *I don't think so. I don't claim anything of the work. It is His work. I am like a little pencil in His hand, that is all. He does the thinking. He does the writing. The pencil has nothing to do with it. The pencil has only to be allowed to be used. In human terms, the success of our work should not have happened, no?*[11]

Mother Teresa knew what she was talking about.

I found this out firsthand when, during one particular "success," I stuck my finger into a light socket. Funny thing—I "enjoyed" it so much I did it seven more times! I guess I should mention that the wires weren't hooked up to the circuit breaker, let alone the neighborhood's electrical system. Er, and it wasn't even my house.

It was a house in Juarez, Mexico, where I spent a few days with my friend Alan Henderson, his family, and a bunch of manly short-termers from Southern Cresecent Church in Atlanta. We'd met up with Jason Laffan, a representative of *Casas por Cristo* (CpC). CpC is an organization which works in partnership with the local pastors in Juarez by coordinating teams from the U.S. and Canada to come down and build homes for families who have typically pieced together their present shelter with cardboard and crates.

That week we worked side by side with the Moreno family as we built their new home. Through Jason's guidance and the willing assistance of thirteen clueless gringos, the small two-bedroom house went up in two and a half days, from foundation to wiring. Now, we were no *Extreme Makeover: Home Edition,* but ours were willing hands, ready to assist God in His blessing.

It is not typical for thirteen people to do drywall at one time. But there we were, day two, sheltered from a raging storm outside and trying not to step on toes in the little half-done house as we labored to build it. While nails slammed, drywall was sliced, stucco went flying, and rain poured on the new roof, I learned a valuable lesson: We aren't really the ones building the house.

Although some of our team had construction experience, it was Jason who orchestrated the endeavor. He performed a few hands-on tasks—shoveling, insulation, etc.—but only when he had us all working together on one project (when no screwups would be possible). When we all had our various jobs, he wandered around making sure we weren't nailing through the electrical wires or hanging chicken wire upside down.

Overall, he taught us. He worked us through it, nail by nail. If we were tempted to view our work with pride, we only had to remember that Jason had guided a group of sixth graders through the same process a few weeks before.

So what can a short-termer really do? What can *you* really do? Maybe the question now nags at you: *Can I really make a difference in the short time I'm here?* Herein lies some irony: While our attempts are feeble, God still does amazing things.

> When Mother Teresa appeared on The Tonight Show *in 1982, she interrupted* Johnny Carson's praise of her work by saying, "Do you think, Mr. Carson, for one moment, that that little donkey thought the crowd was giving him the praise and glory instead of Jesus?"

Evaluating Your Mission's Focus

Christian social activist Tony Campolo has a radically different opinion of building projects (which are, incidentally, the most popular kinds of short-term missions): "In spite of their good intentions," says Campolo, "these people often end up doing more harm than good."[12]

Now, hold on—don't throw this book down yet! After all, I just told you about a building project I participated in. Let's hear out the perspective of a man with three decades' worth of experience in mission work and involvement with organizations like Beyond Borders and Habitat for Humanity (which, interestingly enough, is also a building project).

In his book *Speaking My Mind,* Campolo quotes the late Ivan Illich, a missiologist for the World Council of Churches. Illich noted that crews of builders can conceivably take construction jobs away from indigineous peoples who desperately need jobs. In other words, locals are awed by the generosity, speed of the work, and money for the materials, but the final effect may leave local people with a greater sense of inferiority than empowerment.

Anne-Geri' Fann & Greg Taylor

Beyond Borders, the mission organization Campolo had been associated with in Haiti, recently came to a period of reckoning. They had done many building projects, and though they were not all disabling to local people, some of the projects may have indeed done more harm than good.

They prayerfully restructured their program and now call their short-term trips "transformational travel." The focus is not on building structures but on constructing relationships with local people. For example, they pair a short-termer female with a local female to learn from one another about what it means in their respective lands to be a godly woman.

The mission team Greg worked with in Uganda has an internship program that operates on the same principle as Beyond Borders. The short-term trip is meant to transform the travelers and expose them to experiences that will change their lives. The overarching goal is to challenge college students to a mission bigger than themselves, to stretch them with a view toward the possibility of one day making a long-term commitment.

One of the most important aspects of a six-week internship is the bonding experience. This is a three-day stint in which short-termers are taken to remote African villages and placed with local Christian families. Since few if any of the villagers speaks English, the interns must learn how to communicate. They play with children, work in the gardens, ride bikes to local markets, peel potatoes, and eat foods they've never had before (like roasted ants!).

The bonding experience is usually the most dreaded three days of the internship. But afterward, short-termers nearly always say it was the most meaningful aspect of their experience. Some even go so far as to call it the most profound and life-changing event of their lives.

Back to the Prime Directive

A missionary friend of mine recently made an interesting comment. She said it amazed her how readily we get down on our knees for a non-believer who is very ill but take precious little time to pray for his soul during the healthy times in his life. That struck me as both sad and convicting, since it has

> How readily we get down on our knees for a non-believer who is very ill but take precious little time to pray for his soul during the healthy times in his life.

certainly applied to me. Jesus healed the sick, but it was not His primary purpose in coming. His primary purpose was to save us, redeem us, and restore our relationship with God.

It was not only the spiritual destitution of man that appealed to Christ's compassionate nature, but also his physical need. We all know He fed 5,000 people with two fish and some bread, but we often fail to see what *He* saw first.

> *When Jesus landed and saw a large crowd, he had compassion on them, because they were like sheep without a shepherd. So he began teaching them many things.* (Mark 6:34 NIV)

In other words, He educated them *before* He nourished them.

> *Jesus stopped and called them. "What do you want me to do for you?" He asked. "Lord," they answered, "We want our sight." Jesus had compassion on them and touched their eyes. Immediately they received their sight and followed him.* (Matt. 20:32–34 NIV)

Here the compassion of Jesus Christ was manifested in His standing still long enough to listen to the cry of two blind beggars, even though He was on urgent business.

Christian leadership training is the equipping of "God's people for works of service, so that the body of Christ may be built up" (Eph. 4:12 NIV). Christ is the prime model of leadership development because He has provided, by His grace, specific gifts to the body, and thus prepares various leaders to nurture the body. Go and do likewise!

> *Help the poor because you love them; but don't forget that medical clinics and food distribution can never fully heal a hurting human soul. Take time to sit down and learn from the locals and the long-term missionaries, so that you can learn how God is working to redeem His people.*

You are there for only a short time, so ask yourself, "How will I make the best use of this time according to the talents God has given me?"

Walking with the Wise

What can you do to make sure this mission trip benefits the people you are going to serve? The following are some suggestions from long-termers about the benefits of short-term work.

1. Prepare Yourself

Groups that prepare before coming are better off for doing so. Granted, sometimes there is an imbalance in focus on cultural preparation over spiritual. Remember that the first is critical, but the latter can't be forsaken.

Start by writing out your testimony before your trip. If you have a hard time getting started, think about it this way: If you had only thirty seconds to tell someone why you are a Christian, what would you say?

There will almost always be someone interested in hearing your story or testimony. Don't assume that just because you know little of the language, these opportunities won't arise. Guests are asked to speak in many churches, and there will often be a translator present.

2. Be a Partner

Realize that your mission's flurry of activity alters the daily flow of life in a church or organization you are serving—for instance, building onto a school or working in a mission hospital. Be open to learning from and humbly serving the ministry that is already in place rather than the form it might take while you are there.

It is refreshing to observe short-termers with open hearts and willing hands. Just make sure there is a clear objective from both sides as to approach. If short-termers focus on partnering with the people of the country, both sides will understand the objectives and match them.

3. Build Relationships

Take time for them. Don't forget that promoting any kind of change takes time and relationship. This is the Beyond Borders and internship-bonding approach spoken of earlier.

Pray with at least one person. That moment itself could end up being worth the whole trip.

Worship with the people you are there to serve. Worship is so special. It is a benefit in every culture and language. Notice and enjoy the differences but do not attempt to change their style of worship. They are glorifying God. Join them in it.

4. Accept and Adapt

Combine the resources in the country with your own. Motivate people to help others from their own country. Keep moving and adapting by setting up a communication system with your mission team (homeland and target country) concerning the maintenance of God's goals.

5. Be a Good Example

Your *example* affects people more than what you are actually saying. Make sure you are not just preaching God's love but showing God's love.

Be enthusiastic. Bring with you enthusiasm, energy, and new ideas. You will also receive it in return!

Avoid saying, "I have a right to give this advice because I am paying good money to be here!" That's arrogant and not helpful. A missionary will respond more out of compassion when he is in tune with what the Lord is doing in his life.

6. Consider Long-Term Effects

Unless there is some kind of idea of what this mission is all about, all that the trip will be is a feel-good experience, which is not the goal of good mission work. Think instead of the long-range effect of your service. It can really be transforming.

7. Go to Them First

You go, instead of a missionary having to come to you. In another era, it was the missionaries who visited the churches to share what they were doing on the field. It makes a great deal of difference when the church actually comes *to* the mission point instead.

That being said, please pray for a long-term vision in your church. It helps when a supporting church also has that vision, because then the missionary doesn't feel alone doing God's work in their country.

Bring a good report back with clear stories and goals, both met or unmet. Other benefits are the reports you go back with. Most of the time those are positive! It helps because you bring back that sense of "I've been there, and things are exciting" enthusi-asm . . . plus, it brings outreach and support to the ministry.

> We must first get our hearts right. Only then are we ready to begin the equipping process so that we can take the gift of God to the world.

8. Look for God in Everything

Keep your eyes open for things He is doing. You'll know a trip has been success-ful when someone says, "Look what God did," rather than, "Look what I did."

Getting It Right

The most important issue of mission preparation is *not* whether you can smile after spending three miserable hours in the latrine, laugh over how you acci-dentally told someone you were "pregnant" instead of "embarrassed" while attempting the language, or maintain your composure when a chicken lays an egg on your pillow.

As missionary Stephen Meeks says, if bankrupt bankers held a seminar on "How to Grow Rich," what thinking person would take them seriously? If infected members of a leper colony gave a free lecture on "How to Cure Yourself of Leprosy," do you suppose anyone would attend?

It is ironic that often we attempt to bring others to Christ through all sorts of avenues, yet we ourselves hardly know Him. We must first get our hearts right. Only then are we ready to begin the equipping process so that we can take the gift of God to the world.

Be sure to fill out the Spiritual Inventory at the end of this chapter. As you go through it, you will not only be forced to take a good, long look in the mirror; you will also be readying your heart to share something special about the Lord—*what He has done in you*. This goes much deeper than any well you may dig in Africa.

Dig the well, but also dig deeper into what God is doing in the world and in you, and share that living water along with fresh drinking water. Both are desperately needed in the world.

Building the House

We are tools. We need only be willing to be used. Even though Christian books are penned, the Bible is deliberated over, and mission trips are carefully planned, we can still all benefit from this valuable lesson: We aren't really the ones who are building.

The most exciting moment for me in Juarez was when Jason tested the lights and they all came on. While everyone else started on the stucco, my job (in case you wondered earlier why I was gladly wandering around sticking my fingers in light sockets) was to hook up the outlets. Man, that made me nervous. But the lights still came on, and I breathed a big sigh of relief when they did.

Is it okay to take pride in your effort? Of course! The thing to remember is that in order to build successfully, you must commit these truths to heart:

1. The One who taught you to build is the Architect of the universe.
2. The purpose of building is to restore people to a relationship with the Master Builder.

God has the power to raise people up for His work when and where He needs them. You need only be willing, or you can bet your fancy tool belt He'll get someone else to do it and you'll miss out on all the fun.

"Unless the LORD builds the house, its builders labor in vain" (Ps. 127:1 NIV).

ETERNAL ENDEAVORS

Take a Spiritual Inventory

Taking a spiritual inventory before serving on a mission is very important. Why? Because it is possible to do the right thing with the wrong motive.

Jesus said to first examine your heart if you are thinking of bringing a gift to God. Do you resent a friend or hold bitterness toward a family member? Bad relationships, bitterness, jealousy, and selfishness are all wrecking balls for mission trips. The illness in your heart can spread to the mission group and to the host church or culture.

Contrast a polluted heart with the positive outlook that can spread when one humble servant decides to confess sin and receive forgiveness, expose sin and offer forgiveness. Imagine how the love of God can transform a community!

In the spiritual inventory he created for aspiring short-termers, Steve Meeks suggests praying through the following five categories. Meeks says, "Jesus's name is also Wonderful Counselor, so let Him bring to mind the counsel you need to hear. As you pray, pay attention. Sins, problem areas, relationship troubles, instructive Scriptures, or other godly thoughts that come to you should be noted."

Ask God to reveal areas of your life that need transformation. Call on Him to help you make those changes through this trip, His Word, the Holy Spirit, and other people.

Relationships

Seek to discover if there is bitterness or unforgiveness in your heart toward anyone. List any names or situations that come to mind as you pray.

> *Father, You have told us that unless we forgive, we cannot be forgiven. I want to set things right with everyone in my life. Father, is there bitterness or unforgivingness in my heart? Show me all of it. I admit I feel bitterness/unforgivingness against _____. I confess this; I do not want to hold on to it. You have forgiven me of so much worse. I let it go, Father. I feel the pain, but I will not choose any longer to hold this against _____. Help me let go; help me humbly set it right. Forgive me for holding this thing in my heart. Thank You for reminding me. Thank You for guiding me to this time of forgiveness.*
> *In Jesus's Name, Amen.*

Idols/gods

A godly heart cannot contain two masters. In this exercise you will seek to determine what other gods may reside in your heart and then eliminate them through confession and repentance. Do you dabble in the spirit world? Do you experiment with Ouija boards, mediums, fortune-tellers, Tarot cards, or palm reading? Have you tried or gone along with witchcraft, spirit guides, or séances? Do you enjoy visiting satanic web sites or horror movies that glorify evil?

> *Father, I admit I have been involved in _____.*
> *I was wrong to mix it/them into my life. I denounce the practice(s) and will not return to it/them again. Forgive me for my involvement and remove the consequences, seen and unseen, from my heart. You are the only King in my life; I will serve You alone. Thank You for bringing me to deal with this issue today. I love You.*
>
> *In Jesus's name, amen.*

Pride

Pride must be acknowledged and confessed before repentance can ensue. Do any of these apply to you?

I often think my way is better than anyone else's way.

I am a controller rather than a Spirit-controlled person.

I don't think I have any needs.

I rely more on my strengths and resources than on God's.

It is hard for me to admit when I am wrong.

I am driven to be recognized and get credit or honor.

> *Father, show me where pride resides within me. I cannot manage life on my own, though I have sometimes tried. Show me where I am relying on myself instead of You. I confess that pride has lived in me in the area(s) of _____.*
>
> *In Jesus's name, amen.*

ETERNAL ENDEAVORS _____

Rebellion and Iniquity

Sin is not aiming at God's will and missing a few inches to the left or right; rather, it is deciding that you will not even aim at God's target. Sin is rebellion. We need forgiveness and freedom from habitual sin.

Consider the following sins. Do you steal, lie, or fight? Are you argumentative? Do you lust and use pornography? Do you cheat in school? Are you greedy, even with what little you own? Does anger rule you? Do you abuse drugs and alcohol? Are you acting out sexually immoral temptations with the same or opposite sex?

> *Father, I confess I am weak and sinful, often rebellious. I admit I have sexual temptations and don't want to act them out. I admit I am argumentative and want to be a peacemaker. I confess that it is wrong. I denounce it as ungodly. I no longer want to practice _____.*
> *Remove it from me. Set me free. Forgive me. I need You. You are my strength and my supply. Help me, God.*
> *In Jesus's name, amen.*

Motives

Getting our motives right is critical to a successful work in Jesus's name. Mission trips are often opportunities to do good but for the wrong reasons. Once again, ask for Jesus's counsel as you review the list below, then pray.

Remember, some outcomes of a mission trip can be serendipitous, but that is not the goal. Note any of these wrong motives you may have for going on this mission trip.

Guilt
Recognition
Escape from your church situation
Building a personal kingdom
Fun/entertainment

Father, one last time I come to speak to You about my heart. I want it to be purified. I want it to hold only one thing: You.

Father, I confess my motive(s) to You. I will not go on this trip with impure motives remaining in my heart. Forgive me. Please, create in me a clean heart. Give me the right motive of seeking and saving the lost in Your Name. May my every action and word on this trip be only to bring Your heart to the people, so that they can see and be drawn to You.

In Jesus's name, amen.

WHAT YOU DON'T WANT TO OFFER

5

Missionary Moment ...

When a group of North American missionaries came to visit an indigenous tribe in Nigeria, they asked, "How can we help you? What do you need?"

The answer they received was, "We need nothing. We're fine."

The mission group pressed the issue. Finally one of the tribal leaders said, "We don't need that building over there. Could you tear it down for us?"

Feeling like they had hit the jackpot, the North Americans worked diligently to eliminate this useless building, thinking maybe the tribe needed the land for crops.

Near the end of the project, one of the group members asked, "What were you using this building for in the first place?"

"I don't know," shrugged the tribe's patriarch. "Some American group came in and thought we needed a building. So, they built a building."[13]

The Proverbial Proverb

How many proverbs or adages can you think of off the top of your head that apply to this Missionary Moment? A little knowledge is a dangerous thing? Haste makes waste? There are innumerable phrases that pertain. Here are a few others:

1. "A bird in the hand is worth two in the bush."
2. "You can lead a horse to water, but you can't make him drink."
3. "Love is blind."
4. "All roads lead to Rome."
5. "Don't look a gift horse in the mouth."
6. "Look before you leap."
7. "If you can't stand the heat, get out of the kitchen."
8. "Don't throw a wrench into your plans."

I've been biting my nails about this chapter. It is a joy to flesh out mission matters, and it is even fun to laugh at and learn from mission mishaps. Obviously, Greg and I strongly support short-term mission trips—if we didn't, we wouldn't be writing this book.

However, as Ivan Illich and Tony Campolo would surely point out, there are times when these trips can be a bane to all involved. In those cases, a proverb like "Pride goeth before a fall" hits far too close to home.

I find these issues difficult yet necessary to approach with you. I am so glad you feel God placed this trip and this mission on your heart to the point that you would pack your suitcase weeks in advance. So please, read on through this chapter. Try to receive the following examples and challenges with an open mind, a ready heart, and a willingness to say, *"Wow, that sure ain't gonna be me!"*

As we have discussed, there are significant benefits to short-term missions, and there are some projects that cannot thrive without them. But as with any positive effort, there are also challenging realities. Get ready for the big one:

*All (yes, **all**) long-term missionaries interviewed for this survival guide said that the majority of short-term mission teams do not spend an adequate amount of time learning beforehand about the culture and the spiritual climate of the nation, or preparing themselves spiritually for the challenges ahead.*

Uh-oh.

Do *you* feel prepared in these ways? Are you nervous now that you may not be prepared? Let's take a look at the possible downsides to short-term work and see what we can learn from them. It may make a missionary-in-training think seriously about short-term endeavors, which is one of our goals in this book.

We're going to have fun with some old proverbs and see if, by mucking them about a bit, we can learn a thing or two about a missionary's Prime Directive.

1. "Know thyself . . . else thou wilt snow thyself." (On Having a Mighty Mouse Mentality)

My friend Donna was once asked to teach a seminar on parenting for a church outside of Kenya. She had no formal skills

> *Let's not simply build structures; let's build relationships.*

other than having two young children herself. But she was told, "Whatever you tell them is probably better than what they have." She hesitantly accepted and began to prepare her lesson.

Part of her research involved finding out what the families were like. To her credit, she called someone from the area (now living in the States) to gather this information. Once she realized most of the families had more than five children (one had 10!) and that many of those children were teenagers, she returned to the mission group leader, handed over her materials, and said, "Ask them to teach *me* what to do. I'd rather learn from them."

She later commented, "Taking a seminar on parenting from a qualified expert is one thing. Being a North American shouldn't automatically make me an expert."

Donna was wise. She knew that she could not teach others before she had walked in their shoes. This is the Beyond Borders approach: *Let's not simply build structures; let's build relationships.*

In other words: "Here I come, to save the daaaaaaay!" (In case you've forgotten, this was Mighty Mouse's cry as he pierced the sky.) Sometimes we proclaim that same mantra through our attitudes. It may be tempting to assume that because we come from the land of plenty, the indigenous people of our target mission are hanging on for dear life until we arrive.

This is called a Messiah complex. Don't get one.

2. "All roads lead to Rome ... which makes it hard to go anywhere else." (On North American Superiority Complexes)

One church leader who takes groups to Central American countries still refuses to let the national preachers drive his rented vehicle. The reason, he says, is because, "typically, we Americans are more responsible behind the wheel." Yikes! Where did he come up with *that* idea? Wouldn't he rather have someone behind the wheel who is actually familiar with the rules of the road, not to mention the road itself?

One mission *leader* actually took his own salt to Honduras and advised his team to take theirs as well, because he said that the beans and other food

> *It does no one any long-term good when you pile your riches on them. Sometimes it can even have a negative effect by generating an expectation that is impossible to meet. Don't forget that you are there to support a long-term effort, not ride in on your white horse and baptize a whole city or get them all to recite the sinner's prayer. Numbers are relative; restored relationship with God is the prime directive. You are a temporary vessel, and if God wants His work done, He will do it with or without you. Trust Him in that.*

needed salt (as if they didn't have any salt in the whole country). Funny, every Honduran I know puts TONS of salt on their food, and there is plenty on hand if you ask for it.

One short-termer, a member from a supporting congregation, spontaneously called a meeting of the church leaders to tell them he had figured out what they were doing wrong in the three days he was there! Imagine the reception he got. More than likely they were thinking, *And you are who?*

The simple lesson here is: Get over yourself. Listen to people, learn about them, and humbly walk *with* them instead of objectifying them. If you walk into the mission field with the latter attitude, you're choosing to live outside of the spirit and character of Jesus. Christ was a *great* listener, learner, and companion. And, um—He was God! If anyone had a right to a superiority complex, it's the Supreme Being.

3. "A bird in the hand . . . might get scared and leave you a wee gift." (On Overpragmatic Expectations)

Sometimes great ideas don't turn out quite the way we plan them (consider the Nigerian building project at the beginning of the chapter). It is difficult to escape North American expediency: ten latrines dug, ten dramas performed, a VBS in every village, a gospel meeting, and one hundred people won to Christ. But this is also why our short-term stratagem has the capability for collapse, especially when we don't even speak the language.[14]

Listed goals are good, but only when they fulfill what is really needed, not what we *think* is needed. Back to the platinum rule: *Do unto others as they would have you do unto them.*

Many short-termers have good solutions and preventive measures in place, due to their experience and/or resources back home. But sometimes the results can be complicated. Maybe you think, "They need a playground, so let's build them a playground." They might really appreciate a place for their children to play, but perhaps for the same money you could have built a small house with a bathroom.

Plus, there may be more pressing needs at hand: a woman who needs prayer, a family who would be encouraged simply by your presence at their dinner table, an old man you hold an umbrella for as he walks to the grocery store.

You can't give people everything they request, but you can find a way to do something for them personally. If you inquire of the missionaries or indigenous leaders, you can usually find better ways to pursue long-term solutions that are about *them* rather than piecemeal projects that are more about you.

4. "Give him an inch . . . and he'll say, 'Um, that's all right, I've done my part.'" (On Limited Mission-Mindedness)

In the movie *Bruce Almighty*, God gives Bruce Nolan (who has been complaining—loudly—that God has fallen down on His job) a chance to have His powers for a few days. Of course, Bruce abuses this by doing everything totally for Bruce. Toward the end of the movie, when disaster has struck thrice, God confronts him about whether he actually helped anybody.

Bruce's meek response is a simple, "No"—but he does immediately decide to pray for them. He then prattles on about world peace and feeding the hungry. God smiles and says, "Great answer—for a Miss America contest. Now pray about something you really care about."

Bruce finally recognizes the tiny miracles around him, people that give of themselves without regard to how it affects them. In the end, he decides that the most effective way to change lives is to "be the miracle" himself.

Don't be so excited about your upcoming mission to Haiti that you forget it is your turn to wash the dishes after dinner or help your younger sibling with his homework. Who knows what kind of difference you'll make to a friend watching you interact with your family?

If you ask God to show you, you'll recognize not just the miracles He does on your seven-day journey to pass out Bibles in China, but the miracle next door—a kid who has said "no" to drugs and "yes" to education. Maybe you'll join in by offering to tutor him on Saturdays. Maybe you will be a miracle, too.

5. "Give a man a fish; you feed him for a day . . . Give his daughter a bunch of candy and she'll throw up all over you." (On Fostering Dependency)

"I read the handbook, Mrs. Fann, but I didn't believe it!" Joseph cried as he came into the missionary's house with vomit all over his shirt. "He kept looking at me with those sweet little eyes, and I couldn't stand it. I just kept giving him Pixie Stix!"

Our handbook for this particular mission point encouraged the participants not to make a habit of giving away candy. Do you suppose that's because the organization has become callous toward those who might enjoy a tiny luxury like chocolate? Not at all! It is because the handbook writers knew all too well that the children's stomachs are not accustomed to the sweets. Joseph's nasty shirt and a sleepless night for that particular child's mama were the results.

God repeatedly uses short-term missionaries as introductions to the nationals and career missionaries who want to reach them. They generate interest and approachability. And let's be honest, it is easier to "evangelize" a receptive people when one is passing out food and clothing. But there are countless stories of nationals in various countries who have become so dependent on the "fast food" missionary that their own inventiveness has been damaged.

> Many have heard Lao Tzu's famous proverb, "Give a man a fish and you feed him for a day; teach a man to fish and you feed him for a lifetime." Sadly, this wise adage has gone ignored on many short-term trips.

The team that specializes in free giveaways will most likely have chaos on their hands, because this practice encourages begging and dependency.

The team that allows people to make payment, whether it be a live chicken or the monetary equivalent of two cents, will have a good time, encourage skills, and preserve dignity.

When a Central American village woman waits to have a serious surgery until "the gringo" comes to visit because he might give her monetary aid ("He has given it to everyone else!"), she has not become empowered. She has become reliant on a godfather figure who, out of compassion, has contributed to her dependency. There are many other options she could take, but she has been "trained" to wait for the gringo instead of utilizing her country's humanitarian resources.

What can you do to better prepare yourself for humanitarian missions? Spend some time talking with your team leader and experienced missionaries about why so many people are poor, sick, or dependent. This might help you be more attentive to the perhaps greater need of encouraging self-sufficiency.

You must seriously consider that humanitarian work is not necessarily mission work. A hungry child with hollow eyes is evidence of Satan's hold on the world. Why? Because sin set into motion many selfish, corrupt systems that contribute to that hunger. The fact that this child's belly is full does not necessarily loosen Satan's grip. And although "seeds are being sown," you must consider whether you are truly *planting something substantial* or just tossing seeds on the ground and waiting for them to produce.

6. "Curiosity killed the cat . . . that ate the rat that lived in the missionary's house we trashed." (On Exhausting Our Long-Termers and Damaging Christ's Witness)

"The last thing we want down here is 'Tourists for Jesus's'! We don't have time to babysit," says Kim Wirgau, a missionary in Catacamas, Honduras.

She continues, "One time someone actually wanted to make sure I took him to a house that had a dirt floor so he could take a picture of it. I asked him, "How would you feel if you were sitting on your front porch and a van full of people piled out, took pictures of your home, piled back in, and left?"

Molly Dawidow, our missionary friend in Poland, recounts a situation in Vienna when a team chose to attend an opera over a Thursday-night church gathering because they didn't want to miss the "cultural experience." I wonder why they didn't consider fellowshipping with other believers in Vienna a cultural experience? There is nothing wrong with opera; but there were people expecting them and wanting to build relationships with them.

Sometimes, usually due to insufficient preparation, short-termers can injure their Christian witness. Many missionaries complain about the effect when a group does not follow their advice on appropriate dress. For example, when a local sees an innocent tattoo, sometimes missionaries have to explain that the bearer is not worshiping another god. When a resident sees a girl in shorts (bare

Anne-Geri' Fann & Greg Taylor

legs are more offensive than bare breasts in some countries), it is once again the missionary or local preacher who has to explain that she is not being intentionally provocative. (Or is she?)

The bottom line is, the missionaries and locals know more than you about the culture and the people they work with. It will not hurt to wear pants and cover up the tattoos for one week.

Then there is damaged witness that has little to no possibility of being righted. Two missionaries in Germany got

> *You may need to adjust your style of dress, behavior, and activity for personal and group safety while traveling to and fro. You have chosen to be a representative of God in this target mission. It is imperative to uphold the standards set before you by God and by those with whom you are working to bring His message.[15]*

plastered one night because they wanted to taste the famous beer. They lost credibility for a new program they had come to support.

Now, many cultures—such as those in Germany and Italy—disapprove not of drinking but rather of *drunkenness* (a view that is supported by Scripture). These guys crossed the line and embarrassed their supporters. Again, the missionaries had to apologize.

7. "Rosemary for remembrance . . . stinkweed for forgetting." (On Forgetting Why We Came . . . Not to Mention Forgetting Their Names)

You will never forget this experience on the field, and I doubt that you'll ever forget the names of the people who touched you the most. But they might *feel* forgotten.

It is natural to get so caught up in day-to-day life after you return home that you forget about that whole other world you stepped into for a time. An important way to remember is by *returning*. It is understandable that young people wish to have experiences in a variety of countries, but we as leaders aren't really training you to be missionaries when we don't encourage you to establish lasting relationships in a particular mission point.

I know of a young man who went on mission trips to the Czech Republic from eighth to twelfth grade. He made a personal commitment to keep in touch with each of nine friends there. He writes regularly to them about himself, about the weather, about their school, their families . . . and their faith.

Three of those nine have come to Christ. The permanent mission team in Brno "watered" these new believers and continually encourages the growth of the other six. But this young missionary planted an important seed by deeming it important to build personal relationships.

8. "A fool and his money are soon parted . . . often with a going-away party." (On Swiping Support)

Let's just address this now: *There is no substitution for a long-term missionary.*

This should neither discourage you nor dampen your excitement. But what missionary Robert Coote observes is regrettably true: Short-term missions, however helpful they are, do not balance a real decline in long-term commitments.[16] Many talented and spiritually minded folks like yourself are being sent all over the world for short-term mission trips, while there are many who want to be full-time missionaries that can't raise the support.

So who are these trips really benefiting? If we're being honest with ourselves, the answer may be "us." It makes us feel good to watch a slide show of ourselves building a structure or passing out food, clothes, and medicine. It changes our perspective to be with people who don't have what we have, who don't live in what we consider a cozy home.

In this day and age, when it is quite easy to travel, it is understandable that you want to experience other cultures and hope to do some good along the way. These are definitely serendipities to short-term work, but they should not be the only objective.

Here's one option: The church supports a long-term missionary, then sends short-term teams there in support of that mission. This fosters both cultural and empathetic learning experiences for the church members.

Unfortunately, there are several churches in the United States that send thousands of people every year to do short-term forays in places like Zimbabwe, Bulgaria, Ecuador, Ghana, China, Haiti, and Kazakhstan, yet support no full-time missionaries in those countries.

It would be interesting to know just how many Christians opt to donate to short-term missions over committing their resources to full-time missionaries. It is easy, it is a one-time gift, and it doesn't hurt us. However, it does hurt somebody.

Greg and I have been involved with both short- and long-term missions for many years, and we have many family and friends that support us with prayer or money (or both). Greg was a long-term missionary in Uganda, where he planted churches and hosted hundreds of short-term visitors. My parents were missionaries in New Zealand for years. Boy, do I know about raising support!

When my short-term teams have to raise money, we always experience nervousness that we might not make our goal. *But we always do!* These supporters are big givers with big hearts for teen missions.

But then there is my cousin Ryan, the one who played the starring role in *The Death of Stretch Armstrong.* He and his wife, Amanda, are full-time missionaries in Mexico City. They are good missionaries. They send regular reports to their supporting churches about the relationships they are forming, church

Anne-Geri' Fann & Greg Taylor

groups meeting in their home, and people who have come to Christ. However, they had to return stateside three times in two years to raise money, and they still had trouble meeting their goal. *And they don't need much more monthly support than one of my team members gets for a week or two on a quick mission voyage.*

The last time I led a mission trip, we raised, between the twelve of us, more than $20,000. Did you know that, depending on the country, it takes only somewhere between twenty and thirty thousand to support one missionary for an entire year? And we were only there for one week! I can't kid myself by thinking we did more good in a week than Molly or Jeff or Doris or Kyle or Kim or Ryan does in a year.

Keep Your Perspective

> *"He must become greater; I must become less."*
> (John 3:30 NIV)

I have seen this verse printed on several brightly colored mission T-shirts that teams wear off the airplane. Its prime directive is clear: *I will only assist, not interfere, in the order of God's work of saving souls.*

Here are the keys to remember:

1. Avoid bad attitudes, useless projects, and pity parties.
2. Work out of love and relationship.
3. Make friends and keep them.
4. Work *with* your team and the mission leaders.
5. Steer clear of assumptions—ask if they *need* a building before you build it.
6. Pray a lot, and take time to read your Bible while you are there, just to refresh your mind and open your heart.

Remember, Jesus was the ultimate missionary. He listened, He loved, He taught, and He healed. He can do all of those things through you, too, if you let Him.

> *And He sent them out to preach the kingdom of God and to heal the sick* (Luke 9:2 NIV).

BUILDING RELATIONSHIPS 6

Missionary Moment ...

Jellico, a significantly poor part of Appalachia, has a long list of physical and spiritual needs. A group of photographers went there on a humanitarian trip. They spent a good deal of time rebuilding some poor structures and taking family pictures for free.

One of the women in this group had gotten to know one of the patrons of the general store through their working together. Before leaving, she asked him tearfully, "What would you want us to take back with us, to get out of this experience?"

"That's a hard question," the man said. After considering for a moment, he answered, "Just friendship."[18]

Let's talk about what it really means to build relationships on a short-term mission trip by examining three examples of cross-cultural friendship.

1. Uncle Martin, the Martian

One of the first in a line of weird comedy-fantasy sitcoms was a CBS original called *My Favorite Martian*. It aired in 1963 and lasted for three seasons, featuring a Los Angeles reporter who discovers a Martian when he happens across a crashed space vessel.

The Martian, ill-equipped to fix his ship with earth tools, begins the long journey to repair it. In the meantime, he lives with Tim in a garage apartment while passing himself off as "Uncle Martin." (Good thing he could speak English *and* looked human—except for those pesky retractable antennae!).

There is a relatable human element here that transcends the wacky element: the desire to understand the unknown, to actually have a relationship with someone we have nothing in common with.

You'll see this desire in yourself when you enter another land. There is always some kind of mystery in relationships, a quest to find what is real and shared. And that can be a good thing.

But it can also be a bad thing. Sometimes you'll try to solve too many problems, expect too much of yourself and others, or forget to build relationships.

This damages not only the project but also the primary goal of restoring relationship with God and one another.

2. The Iceman

The movie *Mosquito Coast* features a gifted (and slightly fanatical) inventor named Allie Fox. Disenchanted by the U.S. government and frustrated by society, Fox packs his family off to the jungles of Honduras. There he hopes to create his own utopia.

This brilliant inventor decides that *ice* will help bring civilization to the natives of that area. So he builds an ice machine.

But guess what? The ice doesn't bring civilization; it brings chaos.

By the end of the movie, Fox has become consumed by self-righteousness and an inability to admit his flaws. He eventually alienates himself from his family *and* the nationals.

Like Fox, some missionaries commit to mission trips in an effort to find fulfillment. Others develop a savior mentality, becoming so consumed by their personal definition of the mission that they thwart the real purpose.

Look at how Fox's choices affected his *relationships*. Instead of embracing the differences between himself and the national, he pushed his own point of view. In so doing, he also distanced himself emotionally from his family.

Sometimes you'll see a "better" way to do things. But pushing ahead with your ideas should never mean sacrificing human relationships.

Allie Fox didn't understand the importance of relationships. He was gung-ho about that ice, but not so much about the people—or his own family. Clearly, the Iceman isn't a good example of a short-term missionary.

Look at the difference between two short-term missionaries to Zaire:
1. *Phil, a seasoned farmer, watched quietly as his African host family dug a garden around their land. They made heaps of dirt the length and width of burial mounds. He was dying to tell them how to make rows, till the soil, and plant their seeds, but he held his tongue. He didn't know why they were doing it this way, but he wisely assumed there must be a reason.*

2. *Don wasn't as patient as Phil. He took up a hoe and smoothed out their mounds, insisting, "This way will work better for you." Confused, the family let him at it. But the mounds were there again the next morning. Incensed, Don asked if he could plant his own garden next to theirs, to show them how it would grow. Then the yearly rains came . . . and came . . . and came . . . . The deluge wiped out Don's garden, but the family had quite a generous crop during harvest season, thanks to their "burial mound" method that kept the beds lifted.*

       Anne-Geri' Fann & Greg Taylor

Phil was patient and developed a rapport with the family. Don pushed to get his own way, and in so doing distanced himself from them. Both learned a valuable lesson, albeit in different ways: Developing relationships is more important than whether a project is going your way.[19]

3. Elven Wisdom

In the *Lord of the Rings* movies, Legolas Greenleaf knows he is from a different culture. He has the gifts of prophecy, foresight, insight, and perception; he also has a tremendous capacity for love and devotion.

However, there is one thorn in his side: a dwarf by the name of Gimli.

In J. R. R. Tolkien's mythical world, elves normally wouldn't have anything to do with dwarves. But as Legolas comes to understand his part in the Fellowship, he and Gimli develop a certain kinship. As the story progresses, glimpses of cynical humor give way to growing friendship. It is heartwarming and amusing to watch two such completely opposite personalities find common ground.

I use Legolas as an example because of how he dealt with relationships. Although he saw his culture as superior, he learned to listen to Gimli in friendship and in faith, to treat him with honor and respect. This took time to develop, but Legolas was willing to do it for the ultimate good of the mission.

The Case of Bill and Jackie

Bill first saw the ad in the church bulletin—a team of workers needed willing participants to build a water structure in a remote area of Nigeria. Now that he was retired, Bill wanted to honor the Lord through mission work. He was thrilled about the trip.

But then he found out Jackie was going. Jackie was, to put it mildly, high maintenance. She was a nonstop talker whose favorite topic was herself and her many woes. Bill avoided her at church, and would even admit to making a swift about-turn with his shopping cart if he caught a glimpse of her in the supermarket.

"I really don't know if I can do this," he told his wife.

"You probably can't," she replied. "Not if you leave it up to yourself."

Bill took this as a gentle reminder that he had been called not only to take up his cross but, if need be, to lay down his life as well.

Laying down your life *doesn't always mean the risk involved in mission work. Sometimes it means remembering the most important mission: the souls we go to touch. Sometimes it means searching for ways to walk alongside a difficult person with honor and respect. And yes, sometimes it even means finding a way to work with a person you've been avoiding.*

Five Things to Think About

1. Evaluate why you're going on this trip. Are you going in order to serve people, or is this just a way to escape your everyday life for a week or two?

2. Don't separate yourself. Take some time to learn the locals' names, no matter how difficult—maybe write them down in your journal. You may want to venture outside wherever you are staying with your mission team (with your leader's permission, of course). It's hard to make relationships from behind a wall.

3. Stop trying to solve everyone's problems. You are there to help and teach, but also to learn. One internship-bonding experience in Uganda was thrown into chaos because a short-termer—we'll call him Jack—decided to take on several issues that had been plaguing the church for a hundred years. Though Jack had never researched, discussed, or studied the cultural practice of polygamy, he decided to "straighten out" all the villagers on this issue. After repeatedly refusing to listen to local missionaries, Jack was sent home.

> ## The Case of Bill and Jackie
>
> *Bill went on that trip. And unsurprisingly, Jackie was difficult. But the surprising part came when she got over herself enough to love the people and they, for some reason, responded well to her.*
>
> *When Bill returned, he shared with his wife that it was Jackie who taught him to pay attention to the small things, the little blessings that can get away if you let them—things like helping the ladies chop vegetables in the kitchen. In Bill's opinion, Jackie ended up doing more for the kingdom on that trip than anyone else, including him.*

4. Ask to go home with Christians from that area. Be safe and communicate with your group leader, but trust the Christians who are there to show you around their village. No one knows it better, and they'll be honored that you asked. The simple act of walking through their gardens, asking questions about their village and life, and even a visit to the family burial grounds is a way of showing honor and love to a Ugandan.

5. Try to learn the language. I know, I know. You've got a limited amount of time. I'm telling you, it will go a long way with people if you make a *ridiculous* effort! Don't expect miracles, but have some fun. Listen to language CDs before you go and memorize some interesting phrases. I made a valiant (though somewhat pathetic) attempt to learn some German for two months before a trip to Germany. I enjoyed the most awkward but fulfilling conversation with an elderly gentleman at a local restaurant—in fact, it was the highlight of my trip. When you make the effort, it is fun to watch the cultural barriers collapse.

Anne-Geri' Fann & Greg Taylor

Think about and begin putting these five suggestions into practice. You will find yourself standing on higher ground, which will help you see beyond boundaries like language, culture, or how to build relationships. Let me tell you about a time when I found one of those places . . .

High Places

There is no such thing as privacy in Amacuapa, Honduras.

Last summer I tried to find it anyway. I was group leader for a crew that had come down to open a medical clinic in the small village of the Agalta Valley in Olancho. Every morning I hiked up a hill the children called something like *La Roca Grande y Fea* ("Big Ugly Rock Mountain"), where I would sit overlooking three villages in the Agalta Valley and read a few chapters from Greg's novel, *High Places.*

I didn't get going quite so early on that particular Thursday. There were questions to answer, vehicles to arrange, schedules to amend, money to distribute, trips into town to plan . . . you get the idea.

I promised myself I would take the time to climb anyway, after everyone got off, before I set to work on receipts and accounting. So at 10:30 a.m. I took off hiking. *Ah, solace,* I thought happily to myself.

It was then that I heard them.

"Inchi, Inchi, Inchi!" came four giggling voices behind me. *Inchi,* the general Amacuapian pronunciation of *Angie* (the shorter, easier version of my name), is usually a welcome greeting. But today I just wanted to be by myself. Nonetheless, there they were—four little stair-step sisters all under ten years old. They were clamoring through the barbed wire fence to meet me.

My eyes started to roll and I felt a sigh coming on.

Then I felt something else: two little hands shoving themselves into my own, one grabbing my water, another capturing my book. "We want to help you climb!" they said in Spanish. I couldn't help but smile. I was going to have some help climbing. Who doesn't need that?

So off we went, the five of us, two pulling me up that very steep hill; making sure not to let go of the *gringa* because she might fall! (I kept it to myself that they were nearly making me lose my balance.) Taking care to step lightly, I giggled along with my companions all the way up to the big ugly rock.

Crowding onto the rock with me, they proceeded to point out every house in the village and tell me who lived in each one. Then the little girl who had my book turned it over and pointed to Greg's picture. She said, "Who is this gringo? What is this book about? Is it a story? Will you read it to us?"

I told them Greg was a friend who had lived in Uganda for seven years and that he was telling a story about the people who lived there, but that I couldn't read it to them because it was in English. I would, however, try to explain it.

"It's a book about people," I began. "It is about people who do the right things, people who do the wrong things, and people who do the wrong things by trying to do the right things. This story teaches you about people who live very far away from here, but it also teaches you that God is everywhere, teaching people how to love Him in ways you would never expect."

"What is it called?" the oldest girl said.

"It's called *High Places*," I answered.

"Like this big ugly rock?"

"Exactly," I laughed.

As we climbed down the hill I realized that I had not really told them the story. How could I explain to these little ones the plight of Tenwa, who hated his father and constantly fought to understand his place in his tribe? How could I share the story of two missionaries who went to a place they considered heathen, about their trials and different relationships with God? How their friendship with Tenwa intertwined with their own problems, resulting in drastic changes? It was all far too much for these girls to wrap their minds around.

> "It's a book about people," I began. "It is about people who do the right things, people who do the wrong things, and people who do the wrong things by trying to do the right things. This story teaches you about people who live very far away from here, but it also teaches you that God is everywhere, teaching people how to love Him in ways you would never expect."

What they can understand are six biblical messages found throughout Greg's fictional story of the Soga in Uganda:

1. God is everywhere.
2. God is working.
3. God is real.
4. God is in control.
5. God wants you to love Him.
6. High places aren't just big ugly rocks; they are places in your heart—places where you meet God.

These messages are also found in the Amazon jungles, in the city streets of Berlin or Prague, and in your own backyard. If you aren't reminded of the high place where you once met God, I'm willing to bet that this trip you are taking helps you find it.

I found a high place in my relationship with these little ones. I took comfort and joy in the fact that I knew their parents by name, had eaten dinner in their homes before, had wept with them when they lost a dear aunt.

That Thursday morning, the ugly rock was a high place—a place where my true Father blessed me, because I met Him there again through giggles, girls, and the guidance of wee hands.

> "No east or west. No north or south. Yet no other ground was more sacred to him than this cliff where his true father blessed him."[20]

I pray that you meet Him in a similar way on your trip. I pray that when you look at someone whose life and work are very different from yours, you don't see just a number or a project or a mission.

Take the opportunity to look into someone's eyes and come face-to-face with Jesus Christ. There you will find a high place, I promise.

ETERNAL ENDEAVORS

Four types of relationships are important before, during, and after mission trips:
  • Your relationship with God
  • Your relationship with host missionaries
  • Your relationship with your group
  • Your relationship with nationals

It's not enough to recognize the importance of these relationships; you need to live them out in a way that pleases God and reflects His image. Here are three suggestions for each of the relationships.

Relationship with God

Make time to pray. Set your alarm thirty minutes early. This allows you ample time to pray as well as prepare for the day's activities.

Choose one of the Gospels to read during your trip. Be it Matthew, Mark, Luke, or John, focusing on Christ's mission will help you zero in on how yours must reflect His.

Keep a prayer journal. Write down the names of people you want to remember in prayer and situations in which you need wisdom. This written account will show how God is working in you, your group, and the host families. (The back of this book is provided for this purpose.)

Relationship with host missionaries

Take the Golden Rule to the platinum extreme. Don't just do what you *think* someone else wants you to; *ask* them, "What are two or three ways I can serve you while I stay?" Asking questions rather than assuming is a way to show love.

Observe and then find things to do without having to be asked. Examples include washing dishes, offering to help carry groceries from the market, and helping with repairs or odd jobs around the house or mission.

Follow the house rules. If missionaries do not give you guidelines about computer and television use, ask them, "Would it be okay to use the computer? And should I keep to a certain time limit?" In many countries, online time is charged by the minute—yes, it's true! So please ask about this before you connect and run up a $100 online bill!

Anne-Geri' Fann & Greg Taylor

Relationship with your group

Get your head in the game. Listen to what others are talking about on the plane trip and join the conversation.

Determine to be a servant. There are hundreds of ways. Here's one suggestion for young men: when you see women in the group who need a hand with heavy items such as luggage, rush to help.

Participate *with* difficult group members. Deliberately seek out ways to serve the difficult people on your team. You heart will soften toward them, and their attitudes may change as well.

Relationship with nationals

Observe cultural customs. Always greet people according to customs. One of the first mistakes people make is to travel thousands of miles, then stumble in the last three feet in front of the people they've come to serve. If it's customary to kneel in greeting, as in Uganda, then do so—you may not understand why at the time, but you can find out later.

Sit down and talk to host nationals. Write questions down in advance. Think of others as you build your understanding of what to ask. The best times you have will be these rich conversations where you learn, for example, what it's like to be a woman with seven children in the Andes Mountain region living on four dollars a day.

Participate in their lives. If you're in a rural farming area, ask to walk through the garden; even help swing a hoe. Help prepare food, go to market, or serve the needs of the mission.

WHAT TO EXPECT WHEN YOU RETURN HOME

Missionary Moment ...

The following are real-life reactions from short-termers upon returning home:

1. *After spending a week in the Agalta Valley, Chris and Eric decided to go home, give all their clothes away, buy only from Goodwill, and sleep in hammocks "for the rest of our lives."*

2. *After visiting Nigeria, Melissa vowed to "never again use a blow dryer!" (This lasted for about a week.)*

3. *One teenager recalls her reentry into the United States from the Ukraine: "I went into a grocery store and had to go throw up in the bathroom because I was so disgusted by all the materialism! Why do we have five hundred brands of soap and toilet paper?"*

4. *Ron is an architect who recently returned from a project in Romania. "After experiences that seemed weighty with eternal significance," he said, "it was hard to come back and get excited about calculating the measurements of an elevator shaft."*[21]

5. *The Merrick parents testify that their kids, James and Julie, are usually quite the servants for a few weeks after their mission trips. They often ask the question, "What really happened to our teenagers out there?"*

You can't believe it's over. After months of preparation and prayer, the trip is now a memory—a brief flash before your eyes.

Whether you are returning alone or surrounded by Christian comrades, there is no escaping a sense of loss. The lump in your throat or thumping in your chest verifies what you could before only guess at: There really is something more than life in the United States, and *you finally experienced it.*

You are now also experiencing what I call PHD, or *Post-Hiatus Depression* (a term inspired by one of my former students). You have been away from work, school, and all of your household and typical family duties. There were very few "normal" responsibilities because you were placed under unusual circumstances. It was a service to someone else, but it changed your life as well.

Evaluating Your Trip

Many short-termers experience some serious PHD upon their return to everyday life. This response is natural. Each person undergoes something unique on a short-term trip, and reentry is often the most difficult part, both personally and corporately.

Sometimes, upon arriving home, new missionaries become harsh critics of their native land. I know some who really struggle

You may find yourself wondering:
- *Is everyone feeling the same way I am?*
- *How do I share what I've learned?*
- *How should these changes affect me?*
- *Who am I now?*
- *What kind of personal improvement am I going to make?*
- *Is this going to affect my future* 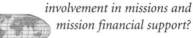 *involvement in missions and mission financial support?*

with resentment toward the United States. This sentiment of disapproval is typically generated by one of two things:

1. **Hypercriticism.** This emotion stems from guilt over all that you have in comparison to the people in the land you visited. You may feel guilty that there is so much affluence when you've just seen children living in abject poverty.
2. **Fault-finding.** This happens when you experience a way of doing things that you happen to like better than the way your homeland does them. You become agitated when things don't change in your own country.

Both of these reactions are common and okay. But like anything, it is important to put them in context rather than allow them to negatively affect your relationships or your worldview.

Revisiting Remorse

People react to guilt in different ways. However, most of these ways are counterproductive to helping the situation. Here are some examples:

Dan, a college student, came home and impulsively made some grandiose financial sacrifices that he couldn't afford. It would have made more sense for Dan to cautiously rethink how and on what he was spending his money, and then make some changes here and there.

Upon his arrival home, Jerry wanted so desperately to return to his mission point and "better the world" that he did so immediately, without taking the time to process the decision, evaluate the situation, or find out where and if he was needed (not to mention *get more training!*).

Feeling convicted about the circumstances from which they had just returned, the Rochelle family removed the air-conditioning unit from their home. A more practical decision might have been for them to cut down on its use and put the money they saved toward missions.

Stacy vowed never to frequent a McDonald's again. Perhaps she could have asked her friends to collect Happy Meal toys for homeless children instead.

Long-term missionary Kim Wirgau recently told me, "Most people become hypercritical of the States after an experience like this. I actually like it when the groups that come here say they

> *Perhaps God does feel honored when we sacrifice a family-planned cruise vacation . . . and perhaps not. I would venture to guess that He is more flattered when we are grateful for what we do have, regularly assess what we value, and moderate the two wisely.*

can't wait to get back to air conditioning and fast food. It shows they know who they are, at least! Reality for them is fast food; it doesn't hurt to admit it!"

The Fussy Factor

Since you spent only a short time in your host culture, it is easy to see the good things that your host country had to offer—and it may be difficult to remain patient with the United States' way of life. Keep in mind that when someone is so enamored with a new perspective that they don't see any serious problems ("Everyone must be this way over here"), that person has just gone on a mission trip to Dream Land.

During this time you have been in close proximity to new friends and, as difficult as it may be to admit, a temporary and artificial environment. Yes, it was a very intense experience, and you see yourself differently from before. This "knight in shining armor" role is invigorating, but it may lead to an enormous letdown when you return to the same life you were leading before the trip.[22]

Here are two important things to keep in mind:

1. **Be aware that the trip has reformatted your perspective.** You may feel a greater capacity for personal improvement, cross-cultural communication, and the ability to integrate these observations into your everyday life. You may lose perspective for a while, see life in your old home as trivial, perhaps clash with others who don't share your outlook.

   Allow yourself ample time to process your feelings. Eventually you will develop an understanding of what happened to you during the past few days or weeks.

2. **Give your own country a break.** There is no need to apologize for your homeland's way of life. Like it or not, it is part of what shaped you as a human being. If there is something you don't like, first seek transforma-

tion of yourself; then, as you see ways to influence your community, participate.

It Changes You

Every time I travel to Honduras, I step off the plane and the humidity slaps me in the face like a sarcastic "welcome back." I love it! It's my strongest memory. It is a refreshing reminder of my second home.

> We go to help others, but usually come away with a greater understanding of ourselves.[23]

Earlier we talked about perspective changes and challenges to our personal worldview. If it hasn't hit you yet, it will. Wait for it. It usually screams at me on the seven-lane paved interstates of Atlanta or when I stop by the Burger King and notice it is not guarded by a guy with an Uzi. There's a *big* difference between here and there. And now there's a big difference in you too.

Embrace it. Find a way to turn your revised worldview into a positive experience that you can share with others as you see what God is doing all around the world through different cultures and different peoples. You were part of that for a time. Now it is part of you.

You are not the first person to have been moved by what you saw. Millions have gone before you, and many share your perspective. You are not alone in your desire to change the world. Join with others in this pursuit.

Share What You Learned

No one can understand your experience better than a fellow short-termer, someone who has traveled to the same place, or even just another person with a passion for missions.

Besides your parents, however, the aforementioned folks might be the only people who will actually want to sit down with your photo album and listen to your stories. Bottom line, most people just want to know that you had a good trip. Some may not be as interested as you'd expect, even if they gave you money.

What I'm saying is . . . Be ready for anything.

You know, they *didn't* go with you; they *don't* get it. But that doesn't make them shallow or insensitive. And it shouldn't make you holier-than-thou, either. It just means they didn't share the same experience. Would you really be that interested in what they did last week?

Yes, you can share your new perspective with everyone, but it may not be how you think. It is not just about telling what happened; it is about becoming something new. You just lived a parable. You have come to understand at least

Anne-Geri' Fann & Greg Taylor

one of the stages a long-term missionary goes through—that "honeymoon" stage in which everything is new and exciting. You have had an effect on those missionaries and the indigenous leaders. You have "done a 180" in your perception of other cultures.

So how do you share this new you with your family and friends? Wait until people ask you questions and show interest before you start talking. Many people either close down or are in awe and don't ask; others simply can't imagine what it's like, and so they try to equate your experience with theirs in the States and ultimately don't seem to hear you. Again, exercise patience.

Okay, so you probably know yourself well enough to determine whether you are going to be an emotional basket case when you return. You have a newly realized, acute awareness that North America is no longer your home. You have left good friends behind, and when you think of their plight you may cry and grieve the distance.

But you will also come to grips with the fact that you are in an eternal relationship with people and would never just say, "Oh, at one time that *was* a part of my life, some idealistic pragmatic church growth humanitarian thing . . ."

NO! You are in eternal community and *love* your new brothers and sisters. You will always pray for them, you will continue to write them, and hopefully you'll be able to make a return visit.

Be an Ambassador

You still identify with your homeland, but you have now developed another sense of who you are. It has possibly accelerated the process that we all go through as Christians (and as humans)—that is, realizing where our true sense of place, of home, is.

You are not just an ambassador of your home country. You are an ambassador of the kingdom of God. You took into *You are an ambassador of the kingdom of God.* another culture the traditions of Christianity, which goes against the grain in many countries. You represented not only the kingdom, but also its King.

The Story of Babel Still Rings True

> "If as one people speaking the same language they have begun to do this, then nothing they plan to do will be impossible for them. Come, let us go down and confuse their language so they will not understand each other." (Gen. 11:6–7 NIV)

In many mission situations the comment is made, "We all speak a different language, but share the same God." Or, "One day we will all sing and praise Him in the same language."

Yes, it is a sweet thing to know that God is above culture, and a sweeter thing still to know that one day we will all speak the same language. There will be no miscommunication, no cultural barriers, no preformed ideas, and no ethno-centrism.

More important, one day there will be no pride. According to Genesis, pride got us into that mess. According to Jesus, only humility will get us out.

There are many different languages and cultures in the world, and you as a short-term missionary just attempted to break the barrier put in place by Babel for the sake of the gospel. You sacrificed time, comfort, and your life on "foreign soil" to follow the Great Commission.

But the Great Commission is not short-term! That commission was a call to follow the example set by Peter, who offered a beggar not just a handout, but also the chance to be healed and to worship God (see Acts 3:1–10).

You're home. It is time to walk with peace in your heart and a revised, refreshed, even *rocked* understanding. As my longtime missionary friend Glenn Robb likes to say, "You did not just become a missionary by crossing the seas, but by seeing the cross." May the high place of the cross give you perspective, confirm your purpose, and help you bring the true gospel of peace to your new friends in a different culture. May you "be the miracle." And may the Lord bless you and keep you.

"So when I am big and grown up to New Zealand I will go, or some other land where people have not heard and do not know that Jesus bled and died for them because He loved them so . . ." (See Dedication for explanation of this rhyme.)

O for a faith that will not shrink.

> *You did not just become a missionary by crossing the seas, but by seeing the cross.*

ETERNAL ENDEAVORS

Consider cutting out this and placing it on your nightstand or in your Bible, putting it in your car, or taping it to your fridge. (Make copies and put in several places.) You'll be experiencing these things right away, so find a spot to put these reminders where you can review the list often and exercise patience—with yourself!

Stuff to Consider Before You Return

1. **Be aware** that you may experience some depression, loneliness, fatigue, and illness as reentry symptoms of stress. Remember, you can experience stress from both happy and sad events. You may go through a grieving process.

2. **Be alert** to your own expectations and the expectations of others. Sometimes conflicts in value will occur, but remember that values are the outcome of an individual's understanding of life. If *you* understand that, then you're headed down the right path.

3. **Be reflective.** Allow for rest, reflection, and rejoicing in what you saw God do. Reflect on your experiences and ask the Lord to show you the various aspects of your trip from which you can grow. Evaluate all that you have been through.

4. **Be active.** Talk about differences in lifestyle that stood out to you (like seeing chickens in a tree), but try not to be judgmental or pass criticisms, even to fellow short-termers.

5. **Be patient.** Take your time to readjust. Be patient when others don't understand what you have experienced.[24]

FOR THE PARENTS

8

Kicking Your Kids out of the Family Tree

> *Behold, children are a heritage from the LORD, the fruit of the womb a reward. Like arrows in the hands of a warrior are the children of one's youth. Blessed is the man who fills his quiver with them! He shall not be put to shame when he speaks with his enemies in the gate* (Ps. 127:3–5 ESV).

Missionary Moment ...

Missionary Mark: *Years ago, Mark Willis heard a missions coordinator cleverly use the analogy of archery in an address to parents. This appealed to Mark because archery was a hobby he had pursued as a youth. He says, "We shape children as an archer shapes arrows: carefully and patiently. We also make them straight and point them in the right direction. But the time does come when we must release them and send them on to reach their goals. I thought it very relevant to sending children out as missionaries, and it has stayed with me all these years."*[25]

Missionary Shirley: *One loving parent, Shirley Jones, was a complete ball of nerves before her daughter went to Latin America. She warned me that she'd call me every week with questions—and she did. She couldn't bear that she wouldn't know what was going on while her daughter was out of the country. Nonetheless, she told me, "I promised God I would give my child to Him when it came time for her to do His service. Now the time is at hand, and I don't want to do it! But I'm going to. He called her, and He called me to remember that His strength is perfect." Shirley Jones is my hero.*

I remember my Great-Aunt Mabel taking me to the swimming pool when I was eight years old. It wasn't my first time in the pool, but it was my first trip with her.

She encouraged me to try diving off the diving board. I told her that the shallow end was fine with me, thank you; I was very comfortable there. I was within arm's reach of the edge, and I had my Snoopy inner tube.

But Great-Aunt Mabel held a trump card: five bucks tucked into her white capri pants pocket. She stood by the diving board, smiling. "It's yours if you give it a go, Angie."

So I gave it a go.

An hour later I was still giving it a go. By no stretch of the imagination was I graceful about it. It was more like . . . flailing. And when I jumped, I splash-swam as fast as I could to the shallow end's retaining rope. But I still jumped . . . and jumped . . . and jumped . . . .

Eventually she had to wrangle me out of the pool for the trip home.

That day Great-Aunt Mabel gave me the inspiration I needed to become a good swimmer. By the next summer I was doing flips in the White River Youth Camp swimming pool.

It wasn't until I was a teenager that Great-Aunt Mabel confessed she was praying every time I got in line for the diving board that day, thinking, *Her mom's gonna kill me.*

Just as you put your children in the hands of good teachers and coaches, so you can put them in the capable hands of Great-Aunt Mabels. They'll inspire and call your child into the deep, perhaps with a little "push," but always with the group's safety as their first priority.

My seventeen-year-old friend James is a very good baseball player. According to his mother, this means that he may have all artificial parts by the time he's twenty-five. He's been bumped, bruised, broken, and slipped random body parts out of joint countless times. But are his parents going to tell him he can't play baseball? No way.

No, this isn't going to be preachy. Hey, if you've said yes to a mission trip for your child (even reluctantly), you, like Shirley Jones in the Missionary Moment, are already my hero. It can be difficult to watch them go, especially when it is to another country and you won't be there to walk them through it.

Greg and I have led dozens of mission trips to various places in and out of the United States. I've talked with concerned parents, paranoid parents, supportive parents, and even unconcerned or apathetic parents. So sure, I may continue to answer the same questions over and over, but that doesn't make the questions invalid. Sometimes I need to ask these questions myself.

Safety will be your number one concern, and your mission leaders should understand that. There are questions that need be asked and issues to address. But there will still come a time when your children "jump into the pool," and while they need to be careful, they also need your support.

Let's talk through some of those major questions and issues, take a look at some helpful examples, and then reevaluate your feelings about what your child is about to do.

Anne-Geri' Fann & Greg Taylor

But first let me say *thank you* for rising to this challenge and encouraging your child to serve God in another venue, out of their comfort zone and yours. It will make an eternal difference in their lives.

Common Questions Parents Ask Concerning Missions:

1. Should my child feel a "calling" for mission work before he or she goes? What if my child feels it and I don't?

It is hard to explain the word "call." This is something that can cause headaches, doubts, and undue stress. Sure, we need to be called! But are we talking about some burning-bush-take-off-your-shoes-this-is-holy-ground kind of call from God? I don't think so.

God calls us by using people, events, and words, including the Bible. We are influenced by the people in our lives and by God's Word—if we're willing to open it, read it, and be transformed by it. We will also be "called" or influenced by events in our lives, such as a missionary speaking at our church or youth group and moving our heart. The call doesn't have to be mysterious; it can simply be a nudge or urging of the Holy Spirit to do something bigger than ourselves.

2. Why do they have to go to another country to do mission work?

They *don't* have to. Your child can go next door to do mission work—in fact, hopefully he or she already does just that (see "Proverbial Proverb Four" in chapter 5). But there are opportunities that present themselves when we least expect it.

You may be surprised to hear that the word *missions* is never used in the Bible. We translate it that way from the Greek word *apostolein* ("to send"), which was translated to the Latin *mitto* ("to send or cause someone to go for some purpose to accomplish some goal").

Missions is a word that has come to represent the Great Commission given to us by our Savior: "Go therefore and make disciples of all the nations, baptizing them in the name of the Father and the Son and the Holy Spirit, teaching them to observe all that I commanded you; and lo, I am with you always, even to the end of the age" (Matt. 28:19–20 NASB).

It is a matter of great urgency that we commit ourselves to carrying out the missionary task. Less than 7 percent of those living today are born-again Christians. About 50 percent of the world's population still does not even know *who* Jesus Christ is. China, a country with a population of 1.2 billion, has an extremely limited gospel witness.[26] But let us not miss the mandate. Jesus commands us to *go!* And each word that describes missions shows purpose and desire to accomplish some good.

My father gave me a special U.S. penny when I was a child in New Zealand, where my parents were missionaries for almost ten years. He said, "Angie, keep this in your pocket and remember that when you read it, it tells you what you are."

He did not tell me this because money was important to him. Rather, he said, "First of all, you TRUST IN GOD. And don't forget that you are ONE CENT." My father's use of puns could be rather annoying, but this time his humor was profound: *You are **one sent.***

The root of mission involves sending. But who? *My child?* Maybe. That is up to God.

3. Will they be able to drink the water or eat the food?

Great question. Even if the fare consists of basic fruits and vegetables, there is still the issue of whether a person's system can handle the way they are prepared. Your child is going to a different country; you *should* be concerned about what he is putting into his stomach!

4. I'm concerned! Do you have any tips regarding nutrition on a short-term trip?

• *Trust the organization they are going to work with.*

If your child is going to a place where many mission teams have gone before, this factor has no doubt already been considered. Most organizations provide purified drinking water and cook with it too. They know well the gastrointestinal issues that poorly prepared food can cause. Trust them. That said, if you're not sure about the organization, ask the mission leader.

• *Ask before you eat!*

Yes, your child should trust his host missionaries, but if she feels some food is questionable, she should be encouraged to *ask before she eats!* I had a student down twelve cans of a national popular fruit drink before asking if it was okay to do so! Well, it was—but *one* can, not *twelve.* (Anyone know how many mangos, coconut, and guava it takes to spend all day in the latrine? Quick answer: at least twelve cans!)

• *The reality is, sometimes people get sick.*

Typically it happens because a short-termer makes a poor decision about what is appropriate for his stomach ("I'm tough! I can handle it!"). I've spent many an hour watching "tough guys" retch their poor decisions out the van window.

There is always the possibility that someone will get sick from the food or water. But remember, this mission organization would no longer have a pro-

gram if people were getting ill on every trip. GI problems are a natural travel annoyance. Expect that possibility, encourage wise decision making, help your child pack her medicine, and pray for the best.
(More on food and eating on page 21.)

5. Will my child be able to communicate with me on a regular basis?
In most cases there is a high possibility of consistent communication. Technology has made it possible to send personal e-mails, group updates, and even photos of the ongoing trip to interested folks back home. However, no matter how far technology has advanced, there are still places where it will prove troublesome to call home every day.

We understand that it can be pretty nerve-racking to go for several days without hearing a word from your child. Here are some good rules of thumb:

• *No news is usually very good news.*
A mission group might be out in a village that is two hours from the nearest phone. But believe me, if there is an emergency, they will get to that phone. It is, however, generally not expedient to waste gas and service time to drive into town every single day so that everyone can make a phone call.

• *Establish a phone/e-mail tree.*
Find out what the mission leader has planned and, if necessary, offer to create a communication tree—a phone/e-mail list that is set up to get the word out in case of emergency. It might lighten the mission leader's load to have just one person to call instead of thirty, particularly since he will also be dealing with the emergency issue at hand.

This system can also prove helpful for general communication—for example, the mission leader makes one call in the middle of the week to relay what's going on, and then you or another volunteer parent conveys the information to others. This is especially beneficial in villages where there is only one phone and no e-mail access.

• *Volunteer to help with updates.*
Being a team leader is a phenomenally busy job. If they don't already have a website or web log (blog) set up, perhaps you could volunteer to help create one or to post regularly.

When I was in Germany for a few weeks I kept my family, friends, and supporters updated as often as possible by writing a general synopsis of what was going on and sometimes throwing in a picture or two. On my husband's last group to Honduras, he wasn't always able to access the Web; but he did send messages through a friend who would then e-mail me. I, in turn, would post the information on their blog.

There are many free, user-friendly programs available that making writing and posting blog entries easy and convenient. It may greatly relieve the group leader to have you offer to post updates for the team.

• *Talk to the mission leader.*
Most mission leaders understand the necessity of communication and the parental need to know that everything is all right. They can usually communicate upon arrival from the airport, at least once during the trip, and then perhaps again when the group is en route home. If you have a rough idea of when to expect to hear from the team, your fret time will be significantly decreased.

6. Is the government safe/stable? Is it a dangerous place?

Even though there is always a chance your child could drown while swimming, it doesn't mean you won't go swimming with him, right? You can't be there on their mission trip, but the same concept applies. You are a parent, and your child's safety is your first priority. The mission leaders and local missionaries now share this responsibility. You have to make the decision to trust them to take care of your child. If this sounds trite, please read on.

You may have heard true stories about horrible events on a mission trip. A Peace Corps worker raped in a taxi cab, a missionary's child kidnapped, a mission team member falling to his death from a swinging bridge, a bus full of hijacked passengers.

I'm not going to mince words here. These things have happened, and I personally know people who have experienced them. These are the kinds of stories that make parents say "No way" to their child when she wants to go on a mission trip. These are the stories that keep you up at night. But before I change your mind about this trip in one paragraph, let's discuss a few important factors.

• *Mission tragedies are extremely rare.*
As discussed previously in this book, there are thousands of short-term mission trips taken every year. Draw comfort in knowing that the awful tragedies you hear about are going to be about one in a million. If you are tempted to say, "But what if my child is that one?" then it may be a good idea to reevaluate what it means to be liable for your children. It might even help to read this book with him (or get your own copy and don't tell him about it).

Bottom line: Things have happened, but statistically not very often. Again, these mission organizations wouldn't have existing programs if tragedies occurred regularly on their watch.

Anne-Geri' Fann & Greg Taylor

- *Consider your local news.* A convenience store in your neighborhood was robbed; are you moving away from the city? You hear there may be a crack house somewhere near your part of town; do you still allow your children to play in the backyard? A horrible car accident involving a teenager last weekend made your heart beat faster; will you forbid your daughter to get her driver's license?

You know where you feel safe even when there are other things going on in your area. Just because something happened on one side of the target country doesn't mean it isn't safe to be on the other side. So . . .

- *Find out as much about the target mission point as you can, but find out from sources you trust.*

Consider avoiding the Center for Disease Control (CDC) or government Internet overviews. These sites are going to tell you the worst-case scenarios because they have to. Oh, the stories are true, but just as the news is typically going to first report the worst stories of the week, so are these sites designed to list every single thing that could possible go wrong.

Find out about the country, but get the information from missionaries or nationals who have lived there. Don't make a decision based on one negative review. Keep talking to people, choose your sources wisely, and don't lock in on only one source of news.

> *Before I moved to Atlanta, I looked up the crime rate on the Web. Let me just say that it's a good thing I didn't decide whether to move there based solely on what I read. I would have missed a wonderful seven years in Georgia! Likewise, Greg spent seven of the best years of his life in Uganda, where the statistics on crime and rebel warfare were also high.*

7. Is it worth the risk?

Parents do not want to send their children off to war, but they do. Why? *Because for the most part, they believe the cause is worthy.* While they would never choose to sacrifice their children, they allow the possibility that their child is in a place far from them, in a danger zone. Does this mean your child will be in as much danger as in a war zone, in harm's way? Not necessarily, but it is a spiritual battle we face—a battle against fear that would cause us to back down from opportunities for our children to grow and mature through cross-cultural experiences. We never know how far we can go unless we are allowed to push the edge of our own boundaries, our comfort zones. Yes, those mission trip decisions are worth the risk.

Relationship specialist Hal Runkel, the author of *ScreamFree Parenting*, says, "What I've come to appreciate, by learning to calm my own anxiety, is the joy of watching my children make their own decisions because I get to watch them think through a decision. These are learning experiences that I simply could not teach them through my words or even my example."[27]

Leaving the Quiver

(Advice from parents of mission-minded teens)

I can't imagine what my life would have been like without the support of my crazy parents, who encouraged me to do everything and go everywhere as long as it didn't cross the lines of my faith base. Yes, I got the missions bug from them in the first place, since they chose to give birth to me way Down Under. They also sent me on domestic mission trips (Ohio and California, for example) as a teenager, helped pay for part of my education in Italy, and supported me at home while I raised money to work in Austria for a semester. Who knows how long it took them to get out of Angie-imposed debt? And who knows how many nights they stayed awake hoping and praying I was okay while I gallivanted across the globe?

So when I wanted advice for this chapter, I naturally turned to Mom and Dad. I also gathered wisdom from numerous other parents who have faithfully watched their kids climb onto planes, church buses, and vans to do mission work in unfamiliar territory.

These parents wanted to share their journeys with you, so without further adieu, I present to you . . .

Mark and Brenda Young
Sending Parents
Trujillo, Colon, Honduras, Central America

Our children have varying mission experience in Haiti and Honduras. We were pretty typical middle-class parents, both working and busy with church work, but we wanted to give our children opportunities to see how most of the rest of the world lived by allowing them to participate in missions in these developing countries. Little did we know what a great impact it would have on *them.* Our teenagers came home with changed hearts and different perspectives. They wrote papers in high school on subjects such as living without good water, surviving in the jungles of Honduras, and how it feels to be poor. We hardly recognized a couple of them, they had changed their attitudes so much.

We give God—as well as some good friends who took them—a lot of credit for giving them positive mission experiences in both places. Today our "teenagers" are all married to Christians and are responsible adults who love the Lord and are highly sensitized to mission work, whether it be in a foreign land or around the corner. They actively participate in intercultural activities and reach out to those people in their communities who are less fortunate than they.

As parents, we are proud of them, but realize that much of who they are today can be credited to their teenage mission experiences. Ironically, these same "teenagers" now support *us!* Three years ago we moved to Honduras as missionaries to work with needy children. Without our children's mission experiences, we would not be here today. *My, how God can use our children!*

Sam S. Adams
Sending Dad
IBM Distinguished Engineer, IBM Research

Part of the biggest challenge to any parent is the idea of being out of control and out of cell phone range without a U.S. policeman, ambulance, or hospital close at hand. But God has a job for us to do, and He is directly involved in both guiding and protecting us in that work.

Whether our kids are in a "wild place" or at the local coffee shop, God is actively using His servants for His glory. And if He is in control, then as long as I follow Him and use the good sense He gave me, His will shall be accomplished. That should always be our goal, even if it be a cross that raises us "nearer, O God, to Thee."

Glen and Anne Gray
Sending Parents . . . Mine!

Parents need to "let go" and trust in God to take care of *His* child. But, if something should happen (injury, death, arriving late at the airport), that's when the parents' trust needs to be in place.

Have confidence that the director of the mission effort will not knowingly jeopardize the safety of the participants. "Dangers" in a foreign country are many times exaggerated by the media and not something parents need to worry about. Keep that in mind and be proud that your child wants to have this experience. Don't stand in the way with unnecessary negatives.

Ginger Brown
Sending Mom

I was pretty comfortable sending my daughter Laura to an enclosed community just outside San Diego, California, on a bus, with lots of adults when she was just fifteen years old. However, I will never forget my reaction when I got a call from the chaplain at her Christian high school when Laura was seventeen: I was told that, after much prayer, they thought Laura should go to Honduras instead of (what I perceived as) a "safe" mission trip to Europe! I was scared about the living conditions of Honduras and feared for the safety of a small group going into such a remote area.

After four years and four trips made by Laura to Honduras, my emotions are much different. The experiences Laura has had in working with poor nations have shaped her personality, beliefs, faith, and lifelong goals. She feels that God has called her to do medical mission work, and she is pursuing a premed degree with a drive and exuberance that I don't think would be there if she hadn't gone on that first trip to Honduras. I have never been as proud of anyone as I am of Laura for her ambition to bring the Word of God to unreached peoples, especially children.

All of the worry and anxiety that are normal emotions for any parent sending a child on a mission trip cannot compare to the joy of knowing that your child has a passion for Christ and a desire to give of all that she is to others.

Pat Lamb
Sending Mom
The thought that fills my mind most is how thankful I was that both of my children wanted to go on a mission trip to a developing country. Honestly, when you go to a country like that, the conditions are so difficult that "fun" becomes relative. And the person will come back changed because of experiencing the poverty and culture, as well as taking Christ to the needy.

Because I was happy for them, that they had the heart and nerve to do this, I didn't even think to worry about their safety—and least of all their comfort! In fact, when I went to one of the parents' meetings and heard the concerns of many other parents, I thought something must be wrong with me because I wasn't worried! Was I not being a good enough parent, to so gladly send my teen into a dangerous situation? But in my mind it simply didn't seem dangerous; it sounded challenging and rewarding, two experiences I wanted my teens to have. And when my son chose to return the second year instead of doing something different, well, my joy was complete!

I was, of course, grateful for a competent sponsor. I didn't have to worry about the details and safety and could focus my prayers on the success of their work projects, medical outreach, and missionary efforts.

Some Final Advice

Let's talk about some of the things these wise sending parents have said.

Often our nervousness as sending parents is part of an anxiety that says *I want to control what my child does so I don't have to deal with how it makes me feel.* But as you know, parenting is not about maintaining control over the activities of your children; it is about influencing them positively as they make choices. You cannot retain a position of influence over your children unless you regain a position of control over ourselves.[28]

Anne-Geri' Fann & Greg Taylor

Look closely at the following "Trust God" acronym, paying special attention the second *T* in the list. I know of parents who say they felt closer to their children when they too were doing service work while their child was away.

It is also something you can share with your child when he returns. You'll have a common ground . . . a step toward better understanding why his eyes are aglow.

Trust the mission leader.

Review the target mission point. Find out as much as you can.

Understand that sometimes it is best to bite your tongue.

Stay away from the Internet if you don't want indigestion!

Take part in a service opportunity while your child is away.

Go to at least one meeting (find out beforehand which would be best for you to attend).

Offer to do something to help the mission leader prepare.

Don't stop praying!

Your children will one day leave the quiver. Wouldn't it bless you to share in that joy by pulling them out yourself and being the archer that sends them? Yes, it is frightening to watch them fly; but you have done your job well, and that target needs to watch out! Your child just may make a direct hit and change some lives because *you* aimed well.

In fact, a bigger blessing to your family, as Jesus's disciples, might be to one day organize a family mission trip. Get some families together and find a mission point that needs you. The blessings will abound in relationships and in ministry.

Now, may God bless you as you challenge your babies to tackle that diving board and leap into the deep end.

A mama eagle will make a nest at least eight feet by eight feet . . . . She will fill it up with leaves, animal fur, and down from her own breast, so it's warm and snug.

But when the time is right, she will make things uncomfortable for her unsuspecting little eaglets.

It all begins when she takes them to a "home" that will be more important to them than any nest or aerie in the world...the sky! She will pick them up, fly with them to a dizzying height, and drop them.

This is all shockingly new to the little eaglet. For him, life has been a comfy, snuggled-down, fuzz ball existence, with little pals to play with, regular meals, and Mama's protective wings at night. But now Mama kicks him overboard, with nothing between him and certain death but the wild blue yonder.

The eaglet begins to flutter. He doesn't know what to do. He doesn't even have a learner's permit. His heart pounds in his tiny chest. And he's heading down, fast.

As the little fella plummets to earth, contemplating his comfortable but surprisingly brief life, mama eagle watches. And what does she do? She swoops down just before her eaglet hits the ground and picks him up. And of course the poor little bird has gone into cardiac arrest.

But there's a happy ending here for the baby eagle, right? Mom is climbing back into the heavens. Oh boy, the nasty trauma is over. Back to the beloved nest...and isn't it just about lunchtime?

But what does she do when she regains altitude? She drops him again! And again! And each time she swoops down to save him and bears him up...on eagle's wings.[29]

ETERNAL ENDEAVORS _____

✂ **Activities and Reflections for Parents**

Cut out (or photocopy) this page for your own reference and reflection.

1. Write a prayer about your concerns, excitement, or thoughts about the trip your child is taking.
2. Call up other parents who have sent their kids out on the mission field. Ask *them* the questions listed in this chapter. Listen to what they share, and say another prayer.
3. While your child is on the field, go to an unusual environment for you (soup kitchen, homeless shelter) and find opportunities to share the gospel with an individual.
4. Copy the "TRUST GOD" acronym from this chapter (also on page 96) and post it on your refrigerator, right next to your child's picture.
5. Ask a group of other parents to pray (and fast, if possible) with you while your child is gone. Here is a week's worth of things to pray about, broken down into a specific topic for each day. If your child will be gone for more than one week, I am *certain* you can think of other prayer ideas to add.

Day 1	for safe travel; health
Day 2	for the people they are going to touch; for the gospel to be shared
Day 3	for humility/cultural awareness
Day 4	for patience/flexibility; for the leaders; for the missionaries
Day 5	for the language barrier
Day 6	for spiritual growth
Day 7	for lasting relationships to be formed

T — Trust the mission leader.

R — Review the target mission point. Find out as much as you can.

U — Understand that sometimes it is best to bite your tongue.

S — Stay away from the Internet if you don't want indigestion!

T — Take part in a service opportunity while your child is away.

G — Go to at least one meeting (find out beforehand which would be best for you to attend).

O — Offer to do something to help the mission leader prepare.

D — Don't stop praying!

RECOMMENDED RESOURCES

The Kibo Group

www.kibogroup.org
Partners with creative people in both short- and long-term mission capacities to develop solutions for sustainable and community development in East Africa.

International Mission Internships (IMI)

http://www.harding.edu/cwm/internship/2004handbook.htm
Places university students with experienced missionaries for six-week-long internships that include a two-night bonding experience with locals.

Harding University at Tahkodah (HUT)

www.harding.edu/CWM
The HUT training village offers economic and cultural learning games to show what real life is like in a developing nation.

Mission Alive

http://www.missionalive.org
Experientially trains mission teams and Christian leaders as evangelists and church planters.

Youth Works

http://www.youthworks.com
Provides weeklong youth mission trips throughout the United States, Canada, and Mexico.

Ministry of Money

http://www.ministryofmoney.org
Offers retreats, workshops, and pilgrimages in which participants explore the issues of money and spirituality.

Youth With a Mission (YWAM)

http://www.ywam.org
Sends out twenty-five thousand short-term missionaries each year. Participants make God known through evangelism, mercy ministries, and discipleship training.

Habitat for Humanity International (HFHI)

http://www.habitat.org
Seeks to eliminate poverty housing and homelessness and to make decent
shelter a matter of conscience and action. HFHI invites people of all back-
grounds, races, and religions to partner with families in need through house-
building projects.

Short-Term Evangelical Missions (STEM)

www.STEMmin.org
Offers training events, consulting, and publications to help churches and
sending groups achieve maximum impact in their short-term mission programs.

Mission Year

www.missionyear.org
Sends young people for one year to work in a poor urban neighborhood. In
that time participants partner with a local church, volunteer at a social service
agency, and develop relationships within the community.

Beyond Borders

www.BeyondBorders.net
Organizes reflective journeys and long-term apprenticeships that create
opportunities for dialogue between the visitors and their Haitian hosts.

Educational Concerns for Hunger Organization (ECHO)

http://echonet.org/index.htm
Helps those working internationally with the poor be more effective, particularly in the areas of agricultural advancements and developing technology.

Casas por Cristo

http://www.casasporcristo.org
A nondenominational ministry addressing the needs of the poor in Mexico
through partnerships with churches in the U.S., Canada, and Mexico (Casas
por Cristo is Spanish for "Houses because of Christ").

World Servants

www.worldservants.org
Leads short-term mission trips with the goal to help communities become
self-sustaining and interdependent.

World Vision

http://www.worldvisionresources.com
A Christian relief and development organization dedicated to helping children and their communities worldwide by tackling the roots of poverty.

Christ in Youth (CIV)

www.ciy.com
Gives youth groups short-term mission experiences that include service, evangelism, and discipleship.

World Wide Youth Camps (WWYC)

www.wwyc.org
An international missions ministry focused on making Christ known in every tongue, tribe, and nation. WWYC prepares teams and leaders to partner with mentors in-country.

Amor Ministries

http://www.amor.org
Offers short-term mission trips dedicated to serving local churches in Mexico.

Adventures in Missions

http://www.adventures.org
An interdenominational short-term mission organization whose objective is to mobilize and equip the church by bringing the mission field to the church's doorstep.

Caleb Project

http://www.calebproject.org
An organization that provides media tools and training experiences to equip the body of Christ for strategic ministry.

Global Frontier Missions

http://www.globalfrontiermissions.com
A missions training base in Tlaxiaco, Oaxaca, Mexico, that hosts short-term missions trips for youth, long-term missionary training, medical missions, and an indigenous Bible school.

Youth Group Missions

http://www.groupworkcamps.com
Serves churches by providing Christian mission trips that help children, youth, and adults grow in their relationship with Jesus.

Life Connections International

http://www.lifeconnectionsintl.com
Unifies and encourages the body of Christ by supporting the work of churches and parachurch organizations worldwide, the largest focus being on short-term missions.

NOTES

[1]Charlie Plumb, "Packing Parachutes," as quoted in *Insights into Excellence* (Harrisburg, PA: Executive Books, 1995).

[2]Anatoly Zak, "Sea Launch Flight Downed by Prelaunch Glitch," Space.com (*http://www.space.com/businesstechnology/business/sea_launch_000315.html*, March 2000).

[3]"Are Short-Term Missions Good Stewardship?" *Christianity Today* (http://www.christianitytoday.com/ct/2005/127/22.0.html, 5 July 2005).

[4]Dr. Michael O'Conner, "First Contact and the Prime Directive," from a lecture given at Millikin University (http://faculty.millikin.edu/~moconner.hum.faculty.mu/e220/prime_directive.html).

[5]Lloyd Kwast, "Understanding Culture," in *Perspectives on the World Christian Movement* (1981): 362–3.

[6]Gailyn VanRheenan, *Missions: Biblical Foundations and Contemporary Strategies* (Grand Rapids: Zondervan, 1996), 127–28.

[7]Herbert Kane, *Understanding Christian Missions* (Grand Rapids: Baker Book House, 1974), 340.

[8]Eugene A. Nida, *Message and Mission* (New York: Harper & Row, 1960), 1684.

[9]Don Richardson, *Peace Child* (Ventura: Regal Books, 1976), 28–40.

[10]Lauriston Sharp, "Steel Axes for Stone Age Australians," *Human Organization* 11:1, 1952.

[11]Interview with Mother Teresa by Edward W. Desmond, as quoted in *Time* magazine, 4 December 1989.

[12]Tony Campolo, *Speaking My Mind* (Nashville: W Publishing Group, 2004).

[13]Ayumi Nagai, personal interview, 2001. (Name of country changed to deter severe embarrassment from the guilty.)

[14]Miriam Adeney, "McMissions," as quoted in *Christianity Today*, November 1996.

[15]Sue Church, *Honduras Outreach, Inc.*, official handbook, 1998.

[16]Robert T. Coote, *International Bulletin of Mission Research*, January 1995.

[17]Adapted from Sarah Barton's "Top Ten Dos and Don'ts List for Interning in Uganda."

[18]From the 2004 Lifetouch Appalachia Memory Mission Video *Fate and Choices*.

[19]This is a variation of a fictionalized account found in *The Poisonwood Bible* (Barbara Kingsolver, New York: HarperCollins, 1998)

[20]Greg Taylor, *High Places* (Siloam Springs, AR: Leafwood Publishing, 2004), 247.

[21]Ramon Presson, "Mission Trips Without Guilt Trips," *Discipleship Journal*, 2003, 135:61.

[22]Adeney, McMissions.

[23]Church, HOI.

[24]Adapted from the online article "Culture Shock and Re-Entry Stress" (http://www.globalawakening.com/Brazil2001/cultureshock.html).

[25]From a personal interview with Mark Willis, South Pacific Bible College, 2004.

[26]Statistics taken from the *World Almanac 2000, CIA Book of Facts, and The Book of Facts 2000.*

[27]From an interview in *Wineskins* magazine, January–April 2006; www.wineskins.org.

[28]Hal Runkel, *ScreamFree Parenting* (Duluth: ScreamFree Living, 2004).

[29]Eagle story taken from Ron Mehl, *Right with God* (Sisters: Multnomah Publishers, 2003).

IMMERSE
A Water-Resistant New Testament

NEW CENTURY VERSION®
EASY TO READ, IMPOSSIBLE TO PUT DOWN.

(ISBN: 0718016467)

This **COMPACT-SIZE NCV WATER-RESISTANT BIBLE**
can go with you wherever your mission takes you!
It's a New Testament with water-resistant
pages and a secure zipper closure—and
ready to go with you and stay in
good condition whatever
the adventure.

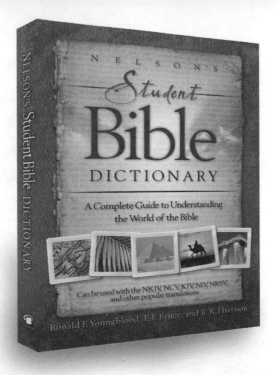
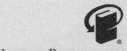

(ISBN: 0718018249)

Experience the latest rage

—the complete Everyday Bible wrapped in durable duct tape! Take this Bible anywhere you want —camping, hiking, mission trips, school, church—and you'll find that the message of the Bible is even more durable than the duct tape! It's a life-changing message that'll last forever.

STUDENT LEADERSHIP UNIVERSITY STUDY GUIDES

JOURNAL

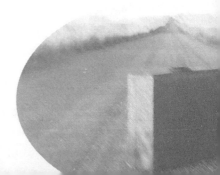

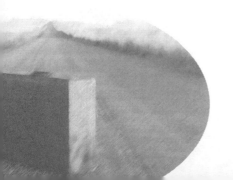

JOURNAL

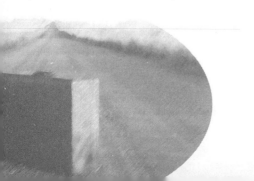